The Russian Economy

From Rags to Riches

The Russian Economy

From Rags to Riches

Edited by

A. Sizov

Nova Science Publishers, Inc.

Art Director: Christopher Concannon
Graphics: Elenor Kallberg and Maria Ester Hawrys
Manuscript Coordinator: Roseann Pena
Book Production: Tammy Sauter, Benjamin Fung
and Michelle Lalo
Circulation: Irene Kwartiroff and Annette Hellinger

Library of Congress Cataloging–in–Publication Data
available upon request

ISBN 1-56072-215-0

6080 Jericho Turnpike, Suite 207
Commack, New York 11725
Tele. 516-499-3103 Fax 516-499-3146
E Mail Novasci1@aol.com

Printed in the United States of America

Contents

INTRODUCTION

Andrei Sizov
President, RussEcon Analytical Center

The Russian economy is passing through a difficult time. The reforms launched by the Gaidar government are making only slow headway and have not yet produced tangible results. The crisis caused by events dating back decades is deepening. It is like a delayed action mine, whose time has finally come. Nearly all elements of the old economic command-and-allocation system are lying in ruins. Economic links between the ex-Union republics are disrupted. The production of energy and food continues to decline. Inflation has made paupers out of millions of Russians.

But, on the other hand, the verbiage about reforms, which remained empty despite Gorbachev's famous phrase, "the process has begun", is finally giving way to genuine economic changes.

The purpose of this collection is to trace the progress and the trends of economic reform. Well-known authors discuss the principal economic problems facing Russia: privatization, inflation, food and fuel supplies, building an open economy, and the proliferation of the second economy, which often means corrupt practices.

We selected our material so as to encourage an exchange of opinions. Not a single section contains a one-track evaluation of the subjects under discussion. They have many aspects, and their analytical treatment should be correspondingly comprehensive. This alone can help form a clear idea of what is going on in Russia.

Taking care not to force my ideas on the readers, I shall only say that in the final analysis, Russia has everything to combat the crisis and occupy a worthy place in the world community: natural resources, a huge and far from saturated market, and, most important, hard-working people. The mounting crisis is a result, not of inaction, as was the case only last year, but, on the contrary, of the effort to bring the hidden ills of the economic organism out into the open. But the treatment is bound to be painful and prolonged.

Prices, Incomes, and the Living Standard

Vadim Kirichenko

Few problems posed by the transition to the free market are more controversial, complicated, and urgent than that of price formation. Important though they may be both in the short and long term, economic reforms directly affect only a section of the population, while a revision of price formation is bound to touch all social groups. This issue has incorporated all major questions of life under the free market: incentives for efficient labor and development of production, sources of technical progress, inter-regional economic relations, and, of course, the living standard.

All programs of transition to market relations addressed the issue of price formation. All proposed a price rise, some on behalf of the state, which was to take the consequences, and others anonymously, under the impact of market forces. Certain programs were unable and indeed reluctant to forecast the outcome of the steps they proposed. Their professional soundness came up against seemingly insurmountable obstacles presented by mass consciousness and the smoke-screen of populism.

Since April 1991, price formation, incomes, and living standards began to change with breathtaking speed. All accustomed correlations of costs in the economy were shifted. Within a very short time, the scale of prices changed quite dramatically. In the last quarter of 1991 the population's incomes rose twice as compared to the same period of 1990, and their share that exceeded expenditure rose 2.3 times. Against an unprecedented rise of incomes, the living standard began to decline.

Used to describe these processes at the initial stage of price formation were not only state statistics of incomes and expenditures, but also the results of the studies monitoring the evolution of retail prices and the prices of services on the basis of their monthly records (done over the past few months), as well as surveys of the budgets of 75,000 families specially conducted at the time of price shifts.

SHOULD THE RUBICON HAVE BEEN CROSSED?

Of course it should have, and not only for theoretical reasons (once the need to revive market relations has been recognized, the price-formation mechanism also have to be revised) but also for purely practical considerations.

For decades the levels and correlation of prices (both commodity-wise and regionally) were badly deformed. Many of them did not reflect the real costs (especially in agriculture, food industry, and the extracting industries), which made it necessary to compensate (subsidize) low prices: in 1990, the subsidies reached 120 billion roubles, that is, about one-fourth of the budget. In 1991, considering the new purchase prices, about 230 billion roubles, 50% of the budget, would have been necessary.

In 1988, the system of complete cost accounting was introduced for all enterprises, and they received more rights in the use of profits, price-formation, and converting non-cash payments into cash, but monopoly was not dismantled and nothing was done about the taxation system, credit emission, and price-formation generally. Budget-financed social programs grew in scope and number. As a result, at the end of the 12th five-year plan, the country entered a period of prolonged, almost uncontrollable galloping incomes growth.

Over five years, the increase in money incomes reached 232 billion roubles (an average of 9.2% a year). In 1990 alone, the figure was 94 billion roubles (17% annually) as against an average of 15.6 billion roubles (4.2% a year) in the 11th five-year plan. Like an avalanche, this flood of money came down on the consumer market

In 1986-90, money incomes exceeded the spending on goods, services, and various payments by 9% of the volume of incomes (in 1990--12%) as against 4.5% during the 11th five-year plan.

By the end of 1990, the forcibly postponed effective demand of the population exceeded 230 billion roubles (with the volume of retail trade turnover and paid services equalling 473 billion roubles). In point of fact, this is the sum paid in excess of actually produced goods and services. This figure indicates the measure of hidden, suppressed inflation, because under free market price formation the prices, which tend to reach balance with demand, would have grown by the amount of pent-up demand.

In 1990, a number of steps managed to reduce the budget deficit from 81 billion roubles in 1989 to 58 billion roubles (about 14 billion roubles in 1975). But in early 1991 a fiscal crisis broke out. In the first quarter the budget deficit reached 27 billion roubles, having exceeded the top figure set for the entire year.

The chase after money at one flank of the economic life was accompanied by flight from money at the other, where people did their best to buy something, anything, regardless of whether they needed it. As a result of panic buying, which depleted the stocks and, in fact, destroyed the consumer market, virtually everything was now in short supply. In 1990 excessive (as compared to usual) purchases amounted to 45-50 billion roubles, about 20 billion more than in 1989. In the families of factory and office workers stocks of vegetable oil increased 1.7 times, pasta products--1.9 times, and cereals--1.6 times in just one year.

To get out of this situation, the country had to discard command economic methods, build a multistructural economy, and develop market relations. Among the barriers on the way to these goals were a distorted correlation of prices and obsolete price formation methods. Comprehensive reform of price formation was obviously vitally and urgently necessary. A leap had to be made after a long period of marking time.

No Springboard for a Leap

The breakthrough in price-formation was to be made in extremely unfavorable economic and political circumstances.

On the economic side, the resource base of the market was shrinking all round.

Immediately before the outset of reform panic buying exploded. The shops were swept literally empty of goods. While in January, 39 billion roubles worth of goods were sold, the figure for March was 52 billion (36.5% more than in March of the previous year). By early April, the stocks in retail trade were at their all-time low, nearly one-third less that the prescribed volume.

The price-formation reform was introduced against the background of production slump and contracting imports. The former became obvious back in 1990, but at that time it did not yet affect the manufacture of consumer goods. In early 1991, it expanded there as well

The year 1991 was also the time when it became necessary to increase the spending (five-six times) on the servicing of our foreign debts. Simultaneously, hard currency revenues dropped due to shrunk exports, and short-term loans were also very hard to obtain. As a result, the imports declined (by 45% in January-September), and the domestic market was sadly depleted.

The price rise failed to restore the balance. In the first half of the year deliveries of foodstuffs to the market dropped by 15% (of imported ones, by 44%), and of non-foods--by 10% (2.2 times in the case of imported goods). While in 1990, the share of imported goods in the market stocks of light industry constituted nearly 30%, in 1991 they dropped to 11-12%. The production of recreational, sports, and household goods remained more or less stable.

After the price rise, the stocks of foodstuffs accounted for one-third of the cost of family consumption in the first half of the year. Later, the physical volume of trade turnover began to decline more slowly (see Table 3).

The price-formation reform was conducted against great political odds. It was preceded by mounting interethnic conflicts, mass strikes, and sharper political confrontation. The economy became a hostage of politics. Political slogans were placed above the economic realities.

The promises made during the 1989 election campaigns gave rise to unheard-of social expectations, and the work of representative bodies at various levels blew up the social programs, which did not rest on a solid financial and material foundations.

Populism is a bad springboard for economic reform, including that of price formation; life has shown that it is incompatible with more radical economic change.

The shifts in the prices (both those fixed by the state and freely established ones) that took place at the outset of the price-formation reform meant their growth. The situation was made worse by lack of coordination in price formation among the various republics and regions.

The overall level of prices for goods and services rose 1.8 times. In September 1991, wholesale prices in industry rose 2.6 times as compared with September 1990, retail prices and tariffs for goods and services--twice, and the sales prices of agricultural produce (in the first half of the year)--1.6 times

The first stage of reform ensured high enough profits (in industry profitability was 28%) and made it easier for many enterprises to join the market. The postponed effective demand of the population and enterprises was devalued (this is not social injustice since the bulk of the means was constituted by unearned money paid out over and above the real increase of end output). Prices began to restrict demand both in the consumer market and in the market of production, technical, and investment resources. The market mechanism of price-formation made a better than expected headway, many prices were freed (for 45% of industrial output and about a half of consumer goods).

But the faults of this stage of price-formation reform are also making themselves felt. Too many prices are still set on the basis of cost and are failing to provide an incentive for the growth of production; what is more, in quite a few instances the price rise was rather an anti-stimulus making it possible to increase profits while reducing output. The use of a price system in which fixed and free prices coexist places at a disadvantage those who are obliged to sell their produce for fixed prices, and the situation is getting worse not only at the level of individual enterprise but throughout whole regions.

These faults persist mainly because the market mechanism is developing too slowly: a competitive market environment, which alone can stop prices growing, is non-existent, a number of enterprises are still monopolists, and the economic sectors that could provide an alternative to the overly monopolized public sector are still underdeveloped. The pace of even "minor" privatization is too slow. While cooperatives are counted in hundreds of thousands, private farms--in tens of thousands, and leased industrial enterprises--in thousands, there are only a few privately owned small businesses. By October 1991, only 66 shops and kiosks and 28 public catering establishments in Russia actually belonged to individuals.

If a competitive environment is not built soon, further price liberalization may become uncontrollable and deal a severe blow at state finances and the standard of living. The tasks to be accomplished in this sphere are connected. For the market to exist, free price formation is necessary. But for the market and price formation to become truly civilized, we need faster movement towards privatization, establishment of shareholding companies, land reform, conversion of the defense industry, more sensible public spending and crediting patterns, a more vigorous effort to attract foreign investment, an efficient tax policy, freedom of enterprise and competition, and adequate protection of the consumer. Price liberalization should proceed hand in hand with these reforms.

THE BASTIONS OF SOCIAL SECURITY

Normally, a large-scale price rise, unpleasant though it may be, has natural economic and psychological compensations: as prices grow and output increases, things become accessible (if expensive). The consumer does his best to acquire them responding to the high prices by working more and harder. Money to spend on economic protection of the most vulnerable social groups appears.

In the situation in which price reform is proceeding in Russia, social protection takes the most elementary route: raising money incomes, mainly through direct compensation. The average nominal per capita money incomes of the surveyed families (75,000) rose 1.6 times in the second quarter of 1991 as compared to the same period of the previous year. A third of the increase was accounted for by higher wages, and 46%--by compensation payments and other social security measures. Pensions, scholarships, and grants per family member nearly doubled, and subsidies for public catering increased more than seven-fold.

Pent-up effective demand began to accumulate once more. Even with the price growth, by the end of 1991 its volume was the same as in the beginning.

In the first half of 1991 as compared to December 1990, the price rise was made up for by an 80% increase in incomes. The physical volume of purchases of goods and services declined after April.

The bastions of social security temporarily alleviated the shock of costlier consumption, but they also swallowed up the financial results of the price overhaul and failed to safeguard the economy against another danger, skyrocketing inflation and a deeper gap between people's incomes and spending. What is more, they even worsened the situation. Taken together, these factors paved the way for a new price leap.

In production, the means channelled into consumption increased much faster than output. For instance, in January-July, it dropped by 6.2%, and the means going into consumption grew by 34%, i.e., higher earnings and the overall level of money incomes were not caused by higher labor efficiency or increased production of goods and services.

PRICES AND INCOMES: WHAT IS THE RESULTANT OF TWO FORCES?

Despite much higher nominal money incomes, the living standard of the bulk of the population declined due to the price rise and reduced output. Money incomes (minus income tax and other obligatory payments) adjusted by the consumer price index went down by 15% in the first half of 1991 and by 19% in the second quarter as compared to the same periods of the previous year. In April-June the decline could be observed in all ex-republics without exception, more in Kirgizia and Georgia (25% and 26%) and less in Belarus and Uzbekistan (14%). The hardest hit were the families living in big cities (in the second quarter of 1991, their incomes went down by 31% in Moscow, by 24% in Kemerovo, and by 20% in St.Petersburg).

On average, consumption of goods and services went down by 17%.

The food problem became especially acute. The people bought 15% less meat and meat products, and 19% less animal fats.

The structure of consumer spending changed very much. In the previous few years, the share of money spent on food showed a stable downward tendency, although the absolute figures went up. As prices grow, people are obliged to spend a larger proportion of their money on food: it has already reached 42% as compared to 36% in 1990, while the spending on non-foods decreased from 46% to 43%.

In the situation of rising prices and continuing shortages, the most vulnerable are low-income families, whose diet, which was already meagre enough, became even poorer in meat and meat products. They consume 10% less calories, spend a smaller share of their incomes (it went down from 14% to 11%) on consumer durables, and a larger share (7% more) on the necessaries.

These figures not only highlight the sore spots of both high politics and daily life, but also indicate the need to introduce deep and consistent economic reform and promote all forms of entrepreneurship.

Russian Reform: Step One

Evgeny Yasin

The Context of Reform

The economic crisis

The economy of Russia and the other ex-Union republics is struggling in the grip of crisis, the deepest the country has ever experienced in peacetime.

Here are its chief manifestations. Production has been declining for 25 months; more and more regions and industries are afflicted. It is not yet clear what could stop it. As the campaign to conclude economic agreements for 1992 within the old command network failed (by late December only 25% of agreements were signed as compared to 85% the previous year), the economic situation threatened to deteriorate dramatically already in the first quarter of 1992 after new restrictions on inter-republican movement of goods had been introduced. Many enterprises have neither adequate stocks nor a realistic production plan, and may close in the nearest future.

The production crisis will not let up in the next 1.5-2 years regardless of the character and outcome of the stabilization program. The chief motive force of further decline will be economic disintegration.

Inflation is no longer suppressed and is fast coming into the open. In November-December 1991, the rates of growth of wholesale prices was at least 15% a month, that is, the economy instantly leaped over the 15-20% gap in the annual and monthly inflation rates and approached the dangerous boundary beyond which hyperinflation sets in. The monetary crisis is a major factor of the production slump and economic collapse.

Unjustified economic bans and restrictions imposed on economic agents are not lifted fast enough. The government passes liberal and sound decisions, but the instructions that directly regulate economic activities are not revised or repealed. The market infrastructure is developing slowly, and the authorities at all levels are obstructing its progress restricting middleman activities.

Entrepreneurship, which was counted upon to help overcome the crisis, is making headway, but has not yet made the economy perceptibly healthier. Rather, it is capitalizing on the faults of the two-sector economic model shaped after 1988: in it, the state and the market sector each play the game according to its own rules, which makes it possible to exploit the differences between them to make a fortune without producing very much. The state has not yet given the entrepreneurs access to material and natural resources and the means of production, and private enterprise perforce concentrates on brokerage, not on production.

The investment crisis has entered its fourth year. In many industries, the wear and tear of production facilities has reached a critical mark, and updating and even maintenance are made difficult by drastically reduced imports. State investments have gone sharply down, while private investments, which are operating in an extremely unfavorable environment, cannot yet fill the void.

The construction of housing and cultural facilities is contracting, education, science, health care, the arts, and the urban areas are deteriorating, and economic problems are multiplying.

As a result, the living standard of most people has declined, many people are bitter and are pining for the "good old" totalitarian days.

THE POLITICAL CLIMATE OF REFORM

The political situation is also extremely complicated. Its chief features are the collapse of the state as a single organism and the crisis of state authority.

Russia's political leadership has to answer the difficult question of priorities. Up to August 1991, the local authorities did not have an independent policy but prefer to criticize the Center and reject its stand. The collapse of the Center after the failed putsch was so unexpected for everyone that for almost two months, Russian politicians had been unable to choose a line of behavior.

It seemed that Yeltsin's speech at the Congress of People's Deputies ended the period of uncertainty and that economic reform would henceforth be the chief political line. But the events of November and December showed that the Russian leaders did not yet revise their priorities. It was crucial, they believed, to finish the already enfeebled and powerless Center under the excuse of putting an end to diarchy in Russia. However, when this was done, it turned out that the Center had been connected with all republics by "coordinating threads" necessary to deal with many issues, including ones important for the success of reform. There is now "monarchy" in Russia, but it extends to Russia alone. It has become both much more important and much more difficult to coordinate action with other republics. The Russian leadership used to be able to hoist a banner of sovereignty for the other republics, to support their campaign for independence, and thus to win their confidence. This is no longer so, and Russian leaders are again obliged to postpone other business and concentrate on coordination, setting up the Commonwealth of Independent States and dividing the army, that is, issues that in different circumstances would not have had top priority.

The Power Crisis

A feature of the present situation is the weakening of the power structure. Never-ending elections, referendums, voting, and second voting have made society unreceptive to ideas of stability and continuity, and the game of leap-frog that never seems to stop in the corridors of power justifies the conclusion that the Russian leadership is not yet aware that authority should be, above all, stable.

In view of this, it would be extremely dangerous to believe that the numerous resolutions and decisions will go into action immediately on adoption even in the absence of efficient enforcement mechanisms and the feedback giving a realistic picture of the situation. Far too many normative acts passed by Russia's supreme authorities are hasty and ill-considered. Old laws are declared null and void, new ones are not ready, the general provisions are incomprehensible even to the part of the apparatus that did not take part in drafting the relevant documents, and enterprises are immobilized in consequence. The new instructions are not always communicated to those who are supposed to follow them, no one can be certain of having the whole packet of documents. Settlement of many issues becomes the business of local authorities, who have neither adequate professional training nor enough time to draft the documents and dovetail them with decisions passed by neighbors. The presence of a large locally "ploughed" legal field produces a variety of legal regimes and complicates the relations among regions.

THE GOVERNMENT OF REFORM

To give credit where it is due, Boris Yeltsin was not afraid to entrust economic reform to a group of young professionals having dismissed the economist who, despite considerable practical experience proved unable to cope with the economic problems of perestroika. But if reforms prove too painful, the president, who has to reconcile the various political forces, may be tempted to change the course, sacrificing the government to public moods. The reformers themselves stated more than once they would give up their ministerial posts should the Russian leadership abandon reform.

Manifesting political light-headedness not surprising in professionals who do not expect to keep their jobs for long, the government does not collaborate closely enough with parliament, entrepreneurs, trade unions, representatives of regions, and political parties and movements, leaving the settlement of conflicts and contradictions to Yeltsin, Burbulis, and other political leaders, who sometimes do this by compromises that are ruining reforms.

THE PROGRAM OF REFORM IN RUSSIA

THE IDEA

The plan of reform rests on the classical scheme of economic stabilization, which other countries have already tried, and includes freeing the prices, economic links, and foreign economic contacts; macroeconomic stabilization achieved by abolishing or reducing the budget deficit; a new taxation system; a tight credit policy; some control over the incomes; privatization, and land reform.

Although the principal steps are balanced, the program has a number of obvious faults. A privatization program and decisions indicating the government's intentions in the agrarian field have appeared only recently.

ECONOMIC LIBERALIZATION

THE PRICES

The idea behind the program is clear enough, to give freedom to the producers, to stop setting prices from above and let the market do this through demand and supply, to balance the market, to put an end to or at least alleviate the shortages, and to ensure a more objective correlation among the prices for goods and services. Having set these targets, the government naturally counts on getting certain results, which were attained in other countries thanks to price liberalization.

It is, however, a risky step, and its consequences in Russia may differ perceptibly from what is expected and desired.

First, price liberalization is proceeding against the background of production slump and, what with our monopolized economy, is likely to deepen it even more. As the first step, enterprises will bring their output in line with available material resources and will try to increase profits by hoisting up the prices for their products. Due to shrinking supply the price rise may be quite significant, much higher that the government is expecting.

Second, a fairly large share of regulated prices (estimated at about 10-15%) can produce a situation akin to that in Poland in late 1989, when 80% of the prices were freed (Balzierowicz freed 15% more), a step that proved clearly insufficient to get the market mechanisms going. A long list of fixed and ceiling prices will deform and create tensions in the economic links whenever these prices will clash with free ones. A conflict is emerging between the fixed oil prices and the growing cost of its production caused by the need to purchase the materials and equipment at free prices; a time is bound to come when the incentives to increase or even sustain output will weaken.

A very harmful effect could ensue from limiting the retail trade mark-ups to 25%: this would obstruct intermediate trade, which is extremely important for the free market.

Third, there is risk that price liberalization will fail to do away with the shortages and balance demand and supply. It would be dangerous to retain the old system of allocations within the state trade network with its nonformal, unreliable links, which thrive on shortages.

Liberalization of Economic Contacts

This step was a natural supplement to price liberalization: one is senseless without the other.

But so far the reformers have either had no time or neglected to remove quite a number of restrictions and bans, mainly in departmental acts. The procedure for registering new enterprises is far too cumbersome, permission often depends on one or a handful of officials, and this provides ideal breeding-ground for corruption.

The Russian draft Law on State Orders also leaves one pessimistic, providing as it does for government-approved quotas that are to safeguard the enterprises against excessively high state orders. State bodies may place orders within these quotas, in return for which the producers to be provided with the necessary raw materials and may obligatory orders with their own suppliers. Under this procedure, the whole economy will soon we swathed in state orders. The Law envisages the use of contract prices, which are, however, to be established using methods authorized by the government. Once such a law has been adopted, reform is dead.

The reasons for such a law are obvious: what with monopoly, if the economic contacts are broken the consequences will be heavy indeed, and the market infrastructure is still far too weak.

And yet the draft Law on State Orders means that in many senses the economy would go back, and this is both physically impossible and unnecessary. That in 1992 the economic ties were not restored is obvious. Enterprises, which procrastinated in the hope that the price situation would become clearer, are just where they were to begin with, for even free prices will certainly continue to change.

LIBERALIZATION OF FOREIGN ECONOMIC RELATIONS

The government's intentions are clear enough: access to foreign economic activities is to be given to everyone, with the system of quotas and licensing to be retained, if on a smaller scale; import taxes are to be cut down or abolished; custom tariffs and export taxes are to be fixed so as to prevent excessive export of fuel, energy, and raw materials and increase the export of manufactured articles. Before July 1, 1992, the rouble is to be made convertible in current operations thus slowing down the dollar intervention. The Central Bank has been instructed to establish the rouble exchange rate on the basis of demand and supply in the currency market. To service foreign debts, the producers exporting their goods are to sell 40% of their hard-currency revenues at 50% of the market rate. Besides, another 10% is to be sold to the banks at the market rate so as to maintain the rouble rate. The government intends to reimburse the roubles spent on the purchase of hard currency by the export tax, which is established in hard-currency terms convertible into roubles at the market rate.

Having abandoned the old and introduced a new procedure for the registering of participants in foreign economic activities, the government has so far failed to deal with three problems: (1) who and how will register and keep a record of such organizations; (2) who will distribute (sell) export licenses and how this will be done (this decision was made public directly after the meeting); and (3) who will bear the liabilities for the interstate trade agreements signed by the USSR, and what the procedure will be.

While the first issue is purely technical and would take only time and some effort to settle, the other two have principle importance and will largely determine the organization of foreign economic contacts in Russia.

The sale of export licenses for the chief export articles is, without question, a step in the right direction and should be taken without delay. But the disintegration of the USSR is making it difficult to monitor the exports: the outermost (European) border will be controlled by the Ukrainian and Belarus customs, and it is a moot point whether a customs union with these republics will be formed. If not, licensed goods may be taken out of Russia unimpeded, because building a customs barrier between it and these republics is a long and costly business. It is no secret that in the world market, the principal competitive Russian goods are raw materials and armaments. Consequently, the new exporters will be strongly tempted to take out these commodities by hook or by crook. Obviously, in this situation a customs union or at least cooperation is a matter of top priority for Russia.

The Statute on the Order of Export and Import Quoting and Licensing in Russia showed that the government had failed to fully implement its ideas: export quotas are still assigned "from above"; what is more, there are four different categories of foreign-trade agents and, most probably, different rules for each category; many technical details of the operation of this mechanism being still obscure, the exports are bound to be paralyzed, at least for some time. And if the issue of foreign-trade licenses becomes a prerogative of local authorities, corruption will grow, as will tensions among the regions.

CURRENCY REGULATIONS

The government has, in fact, taken a step towards domestic convertibility of the rouble with a floating exchange rate. For all its theoretical merits, the mechanism that is being introduced will hardly be able to cope with two problems, service the foreign debt and guarantee payment for the imports.

The servicing of foreign debts makes it necessary, first, physically to get together the required amount of currency and, second, to ensure its rouble coverage. The first task is dealt with in the same way as in 1991, that is, by forcing the companies to sell a certain share of their hard currency to the state. But while in 1991 this share was actually 80%, in 1992 it is 40%. This figure is based on an optimistic forecast of the evolution of Russian exports, does not take due account of the expanding practice of concealing hard-currency revenues, and implies that the other republics will be able to service their part of foreign debts.

The state's intention to buy currency to service the foreign debt at 50% the market price makes one wonder whether the budget will be able to bear this load. The mechanisms linking the exporters' rouble expenditures on the purchase of hard currency with the revenues received from the selfsame companies through forcing them to pay their export taxes in roubles calculated in terms of ECU are too intricate to be effective in the short term. Furthermore, it will not take the exporters long to realize that the state is purchasing hard currency with their own money. And if this mechanism does not begin to work immediately on approval, a deficit-free budget becomes unfeasible, the stabilization program will fail, and the West will no longer believe the promises to faithfully service at least a part of the foreign debt.

Having no hard-currency reserve, the government is hoping to bolster the rouble rate by obliging the companies to sell 10% of their hard-currency revenues. This means that Russia's currency market will receive about $2 billion, plus partially convertible or non-convertible currency to the amount of $1.5 billion. In Moscow's currency markets alone, $15-20 million is already sold a week, which sets the annual figure at $1 billion. Consequently, the volume of supply is to rise two or three times, which is clearly not enough to significantly bolster the rouble. The year 1991 showed that at the auctions, the rouble rate is determined not so much by demand and supply of currency as by the inflationary policies of the Union and the republics (monopolistic rise of the dollar price), as well as by political circumstances, which undermine trust in the authorities and increase inflationary expectations. In this situation one cannot, realistically, expect the rouble to cost more than a cent (in the nearest future at least).

As for the imports, our short-term prospect is a sharp drop in the imports of raw and other materials and accessory parts, without which the technological chains will break more and more often. True, the share of the imports is not high, and if they become 60-80 times more expensive, this will not raise the domestic prices too much. But it was calculated that if the proportion of imported goods in the overall volume of production costs constitutes 2-3%, production costs (when the rouble:dollar exchange rate reaches 130:1) will rise 2.4-3.1 times, other factors remaining unchanged.

In the medium term, Russia may have problems because it relies on imports for 85% of the equipment in the dairy, 68% in the textile, and 63% in the chemical industry, as well as a large share of trams, buses, and railway carriages. These industries are clearly unable to update their production capacities relying solely on their own resources, especially when the prices for the produce (milk, transport) are controlled by the state.

MACROECONOMIC STABILIZATION

DIAGNOSIS

The classical economic stabilization instruments are designed to suppress overt inflation, with their harshness directly proportionate to the current inflation rates. Until now, we have had mainly suppressed inflation, especially in the consumer market, although in 1991 overt inflation also became quite high. Any estimates of the current rates of inflation are tentative and are hardly useful when quantitative decisions are passed.

Stabilization-wise, the economic situation is not very hopeful: the budget deficit has reached Latin American proportions, and the growth of the money issue has got out of control. And if this picture is complemented by a five- or six-fold rise in the price of the basic types of fuel and energy (the target of all other producers), one will have to recognize that the government is giving an additional impetus to inflation, under which the tiniest relaxation of the effort may set off hyperinflation and ruin all hopes for rouble stabilization.

Yeltsin's government fell into the same trap as the last Union government: it does not have full control over a single instrument of macroeconomic policy. The ex-republics are pursuing autonomous fiscal policies, and establishing a top limit of budget deficits (even if everyone agrees to this) would lead to maximum deficits everywhere, because those who will restrict themselves will be the losers. The future of the monetary system is even more indefinite: the USSR State Bank is no more and so far has not been replaced. Making the Central Bank of Russia the center of the monetary system would take time and complicate relations with the other republics, who would hasten to introduce quasi-money of their own to protect themselves against the rouble flood from Russia. Furthermore, it is no secret that the Central Bank heads and the government are not on the best of terms.

In this situation, the government's freedom of maneuver is curtailed, but no one can say how far or whether the freedom it does have is enough for it to succeed.

THE BUDGET

The key issue for the government is to take the budget under control and to reduce the deficit. That the reformers are determined to do just this is clear. They would rather sacrifice their medium- and long-term plans (investments) and the nominal living standard (social programs) than fail to attain this goal. Such resolution is justified and should be encouraged, for a strong fiscal system should be the top priority for any modern government.

The declared goal is to achieve a non-deficit budget as early as in the first three months of 1992, or there will be no hope for the stabilization program.

What could hamper this effort?

First and most vexing, blunders when drafting the budget. The government is planning to reduce the current 18% fiscal deficit (share of GNP) by cutting down (by 7% of GNP) public expenditure and raising the taxes. But considering that GNP has fallen by about 12%, the reduction should be by 28-30%. This is hardly feasible without restructuring the funding of the social programs and labor remuneration, and this is bound to take time.

The second snag is the new tax, VAT. The reformers are hoping that being price-elastic, it will safeguard the budget revenues against devaluation. But this concept, which is valid in the medium and long term, may not work at the initial stage, when the need for a balanced budget is at its most urgent.

The theoretical advantages of this tax are known well enough, but its practical shortcomings are also a fact. Its hasty introduction has already produced a multitude of technical, political, and organizational problems, which, if not dealt with, will cut down instead of increasing budget revenues. The European countries needed two-three years on average to get VAT introduced; in the United States it was debated for five years and rejected largely because of organizational and technical difficulties stemming from the country's size (and this in the USA with its level of computerization!)

The same level of budget revenues could, obviously, be attained more easily by a streamlined turnover tax subjected to some correction (setting only the interest rates, their unification, and expanding the range of taxable goods). The wish to preserve the rudiments of VAT (sales tax) is understandable enough, but 1991 showed that the pious wishes of its advocates mean no revenues for the budget. And due to the very high rate of this tax, it would pay to evade it.

Relations between the companies and the government could become much tenser because it is not quite clear what to do about VAT on the goods circulated among republics: the latter have not yet defined their stand on the introduction of this tax.

And considering that the budget is supposed to get more than 40% of its revenues through VAT, any failure or confusion may result in the collapse of the budget.

The next tricky question are the local budgets. At present, in two-thirds of them expenditure exceeds revenues, and one-third cannot do without central financing. The responsibility for reducing public expenditure, especially in the social sphere, will have to be borne by the local authorities, and they will be reluctant to make any cuts affecting the residents' welfare. What is more, gaining a right to regulate the prices and pay out additional compensation to the population, they will certainly use it. Aware of what is happening in the Union republics, they will insist on a single-channel taxation system, reducing the funding of "strange" projects and levying more taxes on enterprises.

Also worrying is the sharp, three-four time reduction of the state's investment programs and arms purchases (by 70%) and the hope to gain early benefits from these steps. On the one hands, many construction projects and defense factories cannot be closed down without first conserving them, which would necessitate considerable expense precisely in the beginning of the year. On the other, the costs will have to be shared among the industries, and as the system of sectoral ministries has collapsed, this will take a long time and be costly; furthermore, unemployment grants will have to be paid, and the social costs are bound to be high.

And, finally, relations among the ex-Union republics are so indefinite that most inter-regional programs will hang "in mid-air".

THE MONETARY SYSTEM

The government's intention to restrict the money issue is theoretically absolutely sound but not easy to carry out in practical terms. First, there is no clear idea about the present volume of money supply and the geographical boundaries within which is should be controlled. Second, due to the Center raising the basic prices, the money supply will have to grow within some unknown limits necessary to service the needs of turnover. Third, this step can be taken only if the ex-republics recognize the reconstruction of the Central Bank of the USSR.

Grave concern is caused by the unilateral transformation of the Central Bank of Russia into the principal bank of the rouble zone. Reform of the banking system will have to address two political problems. First, the other republics must agree to such changes, restricting the budget deficits, etc., and their experts should receive at least basic training. Second, freezing their accounts (including those of enterprises) as a sanction against the republics violating the agreed-on restrictions is not only a double- but a treble-edged step: the republic in question is punished, the enterprises are punished even more severely (for the state's policy which is not their fault), economic ties break, and, as the oil blockade of the Baltics has shown, the self-appointed judge also sustains considerable losses.

The stabilization program is threatened by the abolition of a single center of money issue (introduction of quasi-money). Republican reusable coupons and "private money" (commercial bank certificates) are already in use; the next step would be "local" currencies. This would thwart the Russian government's efforts to stabilize the rouble, and plans for a Russian currency reform as a necessary condition of economic stabilization would again come to the fore.

INCOMES POLICY

The Russian reformers decided to lift all restrictions on labor remuneration in the non-state sector of the economy, making this decision public six weeks before the prices were to be freed. But the government also took a rigid enough stand on the incomes in the budget-financed sector and the pensions, having raised them by 90% as of January 1, 1992.

The rapid and considerable deterioration of the relative material status of the workers in the budget-financed sector will liven up strike action, which is impossible to suppress. And the claims of these social groups can be met only by increasing public spending, which is contrary to the reformers' plans.

RUSSIA AND THE OTHER COMMONWEALTH STATES

In 1991, economic relations among the former Union republics developed extremely unfavorably. Disintegration was caused mainly by two groups of factors: (1) the wish to become independent, to shake off the Center's patronage, even by taking economically destructive steps; (2) the collapse of the fiscal and monetary system, inflation caused by the rapidly growing budget deficits and the shortages of goods and services, which increased correspondingly.

Since the end of 1990, Russia has been making a particularly noticeable "contribution" to the collapse of the old fiscal and monetary system: in its struggle against the Center it used measures that sharply increased the budget deficit and, in the long run, damaged the interests of other republics. The latter lost no time retaliating by restricting the movement of goods, coupons, etc. But, of course, Russia's regions have behaved in exactly the same way towards one another.

After the August events, which speeded up disintegration, an attempt was made to combat these trends and place cooperation on a new basis. An Agreement on Economic Union was signed, and a packet of documents was drawn up to elaborate it. But this work also proved futile. Both bilateral agreements between republics and lower-level ones are constantly violated because the issue of economic cooperation has not been settled at the political level.

TWO STANDS

The first says that Russia's interests demand that it should isolate itself from the other republics to provide a more favorable environment for reform and go over to "equivalent' exchange with them based on world prices, at least as concerns the key goods. The chief argument in favor of such policy is that in the domestic exchanges, Russia sells (oil, gas) at lower-than -world while buying at relatively higher prices (grain, meat, sugar). The premise is that if economic reform is the top priority, anything goes that promotes it, even a harsh policy including building customs barriers along the Russian borders and steps compelling the other republics to introduce national currencies.

Adherents of this stand believe that reaching agreement with the ex-republics may take so long and be so difficult that it would be too late to do anything about economic reform in Russia.

Other analysts are convinced that the advantages Russia could gain from isolation would be illusory, even if various estimates are promising a great deal. Take the Comecon. Forecasts indicated that the USSR would benefit from going over to convertible-currency transactions, while in actual fact it turned out to be in debt, and trade between the member-states dropped by 60% undermining production both in Russia and in the Eastern European states. And the nature of the links among the ex-Union republics is such that the damage may be much greater.

The level of integration in the ex-USSR is much higher due to command economic methods and concentration and monopolization of production. The damage done by the rupture of economic ties is directly proportional to the share of inter-republican exchanges in the volume of production and consumption. Stopping the deliveries of certain types of goods that figure prominently in the turnover may produce a chain reaction of failures in the technological chains. The process is already under way, and if it goes beyond certain boundaries, a catastrophe will ensue.

Advocates of close cooperation among the republics also stress that most "local" goods are not competitive in the world market, and that producers and consumers inside the former USSR need each other. They also note the long-term advantages of a single currency system and the dangers of its quick and spontaneous break-up under crisis. The introduction of reusable coupons in several republics means a step in this dangerous direction; this is a sign that national currencies are coming. At the same time, after the Belovezhsky Treaty, which states that a single currency system is to be preserved in the nearest future and that national currencies can be introduced only by special agreement, purposeful effort is needed to stop the disintegration and avert its adverse effect.

THE MIDDLE WAY

Life shows that the ideas of the Agreement on Economic Union cannot at present be implemented: not all republics want strong supranational institutions. But complete economic independence would obviously cost too much and put in question the success of reform. In this situation, the best way is the middle one, which can be described by referring to Russia as the motive force of reform. It implies that in the Commonwealth of Independent States the chief impetus to reform is given by Russia, which spurs the others on while doing its best to ensure coordinated action and avoid conflicts, and initiates not only reforms but their coordinated introduction with due account for the "local color" of each Commonwealth member.

A civilized interstate dialogue is, in the present situation, a major tool of economic policy if, of course, the crisis leaves room for it. As the old Center weakens and disappears, Russia has to assume special functions, those of the new Center.

Russia's unilateral steps to free the prices were not welcomed by Ukraine and Belarus; the Ukrainian prime minister even urged the Ukrainian farmers not to take meat to Russia or sell it in the market for roubles but to wait for the grivna. The chance for compromise was missed and another step towards disintegration made, probably in the belief that unity would promote the interests of Russia alone. In the meantime, compromise could be reached, and not by postponing price liberalization yet again but by redistributing the newly issued cash, which is what the republics demanded. At the moment, no time must be lost defining the terms of the introduction of national currencies. The coupons in Ukraine are undoubtedly an attempt to introduce parallel money on a unilateral basis and to the detriment of Russia, although, as has been noted, Russia itself did a great deal to propel the Ukrainian government towards this decision.

Ignoring the political equality of the other republics, Russia would only fan up ethnic resentment, and the resistance to its line, even if unsupported by economic arguments, will be desperate and unpredictable due to its irrationality.

The dominant role of Russia is a fact which precludes complete equality in the Commonwealth. Russia must make a convincing effort and avoid a patronizing attitude at all costs to prove to its partners that it is ready to respect their interests, and that their staying within its sphere of influence will not prejudice their dignity and sovereignty but will be advantageous all round.

The Territorial Aspect of Russian Reforms

The behavior of regions and ethnic territories inside Russia shows that disintegration is not likely to stop at the Union level. A new factor is the claim of regions (as administrative territorial units) to equal rights with the autonomous territories and the status of subjects of the federation. Particularly active are the regions possessing considerable resources (raw materials, foodstuffs): they are clamoring for more rights, which will have to be taken away from the Russian bodies of state authority and administration.

In the prevailing situation, several behavioral patterns are likely; the choice of the region in question will depend on its economic potential. Here are the possibilities (implied under region is not only individual regions but also their groups, as well as ethnic territories).

Regions with a strong agrarian sector, where enough (or even more than enough) food is produced to satisfy local needs and which will be able to provided for themselves even under crisis by somewhat reducing consumption and curtailing inter-regional economic ties. They will want to go over to barter with industrialized regions, build up stocks of foodstuffs for this purpose, and simultaneously prohibit or restrict the export of agricultural produce without first obtaining permission from the local authorities. To protect the market, they will restrict the money issue, which is, for the time being, the prerogative of the Union and republican governments. This will probably be done by resorting to ersatz-money (coupons, rationing cards).

Industrialized regions, which do not produce enough food to satisfy their needs at even a minimum level. These regions will look for domestically produced goods that could be bartered for agricultural produce or sold abroad for hard currency. This situation is conducive to structural shifts, as a result of which a market infrastructure will be built, favorable conditions for foreign investments provided, and joint ventures set up. But since such shifts are bound to take time, these regions will have the largest unemployed and partially employed population, and a high likelihood of large-scale social conflicts.

These plans may be hampered by the collapse of the infrastructure, which is already unable to provide for the needs of enterprises; in the very near future, when the transport and communication networks will be destroyed, the situation may worsen. The best off will be the peripheral regions, such as Eastern Siberia and the Far East, which have good reason to press for economic and political secession (considerable natural resources, proximity of foreign capital, convenient export and import channels).

Regions with developed extracting industries and backward agriculture will try to arrange barter with both industrialized and agricultural regions and districts. A special place will belong to the export of raw materials and semi-finished products.

If agricultural output diminishes by about 50 million tons as compared to last year, the regions may start behaving more aggressively and isolationist trends may begin to strengthen.

The agricultural regions will do their best to sell less grain to the state and reduce deliveries of the agricultural produce to be put in storage to other regions in the hope that the prices will go up.

As a result of such behavior, inter-regional tensions may reach a critical point causing an economic war: capitalizing on their monopoly in the production of certain types of fuel and energy, some extracting and industrialized regions may first try to set the prices in their barter with rural areas and, failing, resort to extremely unpopular measures under the threat of social disturbances.

THE SOCIAL CONSEQUENCES OF REFORM

Judging by the results of sociological surveys, the population is now more ready to accept the price rise caused by their liberalization than three months ago. People hope that after the prices have been freed things will be available if more expensive. But if the price rise will not fill the shops with goods, people will consider themselves robbed by the state yet again.

Under the impact of the political leaders' promises, public mentality has shaped a dangerous stereotype: we must be patient until autumn, and will live happily ever after. Public opinion polls show that the majority is prepared to put up with privations for another year, not longer.

The income structure, which indicates the level of social tensions, is not yet explosive (by international standards) in a single ex-Union republic. But reform will widen the income gap thus aggravating the situation. This will be more noticeable in big cities, where the opportunities for making more money are far from equal, and less obvious in the countryside due to a high share of "in kind" incomes.

One cannot but feel anxious about the state of the social security system in Russia. As a result of price liberalization and the policy of macroeconomic stabilization, the living standard of a large proportion of the population will plummet. Unemployment may become considerable, because investments have been all but suppressed, public spending on capital and housing construction, as well as on armaments, is going down, and an efficient program of conversion is absent.

The level of social tensions already differs quite significantly by economic sector and region, being the highest in industry and lowest in agriculture. The most organized and at the same time underprivileged groups will include the miners, the petroleum industry workers, and the railway and civil aviation personnel (the areas where the prices are controlled by the state). It is these professional groups that are likely to become involved in social conflicts. And if their wages are raised, strike action may be launched by teachers, the medical profession, and employees of other budget-financed branches.

POSSIBLE ECONOMIC SCENARIOS

The outcome of reform begun in Russia on January 1, 1992 cannot be predicted with complete certainty. But bearing in mind what has been said above, several (tentative enough) scenarios can be outlined if, of course, the present government remains in office.

SCENARIO ONE (OPTIMISTIC)

The government has managed to carry all its plans through. A tight macroeconomic policy is faithfully pursued: the budget deficit is abolished, the government and the Central Bank reach an agreement on a rigid credit policy, which is consistently implemented, the government does not succumb to the numerous demands to raise incomes and pay out compensation.

The consumer market has become relatively saturated, the shops are offering a decent range of goods sold mainly at free prices. The living standard and the volume of physical consumption has dropped by 15-20%.

The shortages have not disappear altogether, because the production decline not only continues but is getting worse even if the overall trend appears encouraging.

It would be ideal if scarcity of money and lack of opportunity to increase incomes by raising prices due to reduced demand made the producers increase output and the sales of their produce. Moderate inflation would, in this case, provide additional incentives for production. But an attempt to increase or even sustain a certain production level will come up against the shortage of raw and other materials, and so the hopeful signs that may appear in certain industries would not signify much.

It is not very likely that the failure to strengthen contract relations in late 1991 will be offset by enterprises drawing on their own reserves and making an independent effort to find the necessary resources; even if they do, the drop in output in the first quarter of 1992 will be about 10-15% of the November-December level.

The consumer market may improve thanks to the imports paid for with credits and to humanitarian aid, but this is true only of big cities and certain other regions, and will be felt only in five or six months in any case.

If the foreign economic and monetary programs are carried through, imports will grow, as will the supply of convertible currency in the market; as a result, the rouble rate should go up. But, due to the impact of political factors and the overall inflationary situation, this rise will be fall far short of what is desired. At best, it will stabilize at 40-50 roubles per dollar by the summer of 1992.

Events could evolve in this direction if the Commonwealth members reach banking and fiscal agreements (reducing the budget deficit, the crediting of public expenditure) and work out a coordinated money emission policy for the time of transition to reusable coupons or national currencies. Another condition is adhering to the schedule of inter-regional deliveries and refraining from building new barriers to the movement of goods between states and regions. A successful restrictive monetary policy may reduce barter, re-channel some of the flow of goods from the allocation network to the market, and strengthen monetary relations.

But condensed stabilizing measures tightened towards the end of the first quarter can produce a bad deflationary shock aggravated by the rupture of economic links and manifesting itself in the difficulties enterprises have selling their produce, numerous bankruptcies, and rapidly rising unemployment. The shock will be at its worst in the defense and other industries whose chief client is the state. Its adverse effects may be too much for the economy, what with its critical state, and out balance the advantages of a more stable fiscal situation, which can make themselves felt later.

This scenario promises great hardships for the people (the living standard would decline) and is fraught with social discontent. And, although this is the best way to regain economic balance, it will hardly be enacted, requiring as it does an environment that is well nigh impossible to provide.

SCENARIO TWO (PESSIMISTIC)

It rests on the assumption that the government fails to get its plans implemented. Price liberalization would then boil down to a price rise controlled, if not by the state, then by monopoly producers. The shortages would persist, and the market would remain empty. The price rise would be accompanied by a decline in output; producers would refuse to sell so as to prevent the market from regaining balance and to perpetuate the shortages.

A deficit-free budget would prove hard to attain; what is more, public expenditure would have to be increased under pressure, the taxation system would fail, and the budget deficit would grow, compelling the state to increase the issue of money to finance public expenditure. The fiscal situation would be further complicated by the separatist policies of the regions and especially republics within the Russian Federation, the central government no longer being able to control the local authorities.

Faced with more and more insistent demands to raise the wages, pensions, and other money incomes the government would be likely to give in so as to avert large-scale social conflicts, and this means that inflation will continue to increase and may become hyperinflation.

Money would cease to mean anything, and barter would become common practice, taking society back to the most primitive, in-kind economic system. The destruction of productive forces may reach the scope of the civil war years (1918-1921).

The government can stop hyperinflation either by freezing the prices, which would ruin reform (if the prices would remain unchanged for a lengthy period), or by further tightening the fiscal screws (granting that this can be done at all), which could halt all economic activity or force it underground.

Both versions are more than likely to aggravate the social conflicts and expand the use of violence, to increase local isolation, up to Russia's disintegration, and ultimately to result in a defeat of the democratic forces.

SCENARIO THREE (REALISTIC)

The first two scenarios should be regarded as the extremes in the range of possible turns reform could take. In the present situation, neither is likely to be enacted in its pure form, the middle road will most probably be chosen. How extreme the situation will become depends both on the economy's inner characteristics and the decisions of the government, and the latter's ability to implement them. Here is what most analysts believe will happen in this case.

Macroeconomic stabilization is clearly not a near-term prospect. The chief way to reduce the budget deficit is to directly cut down public expenditure.

Credits will become more and more expensive, but the interest rates will lag behind inflation, and it will prove impossible to drastically reduce the issue of money. Many enterprises will be unable to get bank loans.

Russia's economic relations with the other Commonwealth states will not be easy, especially in the matter of mutual deliveries (none of the parties will honor their commitments in a situation of production decline), and coordination of fiscal, credit and monetary policy. The scarcity of cash, which is currently acute, will cease to be a problem generally but will remain so regionally. The barriers in the way of material flows, the contest to win the inflation race, and preparations for the introduction of national currencies will all continue until macroeconomic stabilization has been achieved. But it is just these phenomena that will make this difficult.

The policies of the Russian leadership vs the ex-republics will probably become more and more selective, from close integration with Belarus and Kazakhstan to aloofness (including different currencies) towards Ukraine.

This will help even out the economic level and reduce the shortages, thus undermining the producer's diktat.

Inflation will run at 8-15% a month (250-500% a year). The liberalization of consumer prices will not produce the same results as in the other countries: the shops will not be filled with goods, panic buying will continue against the background of rapid price rises due to reduced production, and the monopolistic administrative structures will pile up goods so as to keep the allocation system alive and retain their advantageous position. The situation in the consumer market may somewhat improve if reform blasts the retail trade monopoly by "flooding" the big cities with consumer goods (using foreign aid among other things) and especially food; speeding up privatization of retail and wholesale trade; and making selling and buying completely free. But a breakthrough will not occur until the fiscal system has been stabilized, and this is unlikely to happen before mid-1993.

Reform of the foreign-economic and currency spheres will probably produce a further drop in our exports, due, among other things, to high export taxes and the exporters having to sell hard currency to the state on disadvantageous terms. Despite the bans, they will do their best to stash their hard-currency earnings in foreign banks. The servicing of foreign debt will remain a sensitive issue both for Russia and the West despite the Big Seven agreeing to debtor's delay.

The growing scarcity of hard currency will make it difficult to make the rouble convertible for current transactions, which is urgently necessary to stop the growth of prices, which are already taking their "cue" from the dollar price converted into roubles. "Dollarization" of the economy will be impossible to prevent. In the domestic market, foreign goods and companies will not provide serious competition for the native monopoly producers, who will still be able to dictate their terms. Large-scale foreign investments are not likely.

However, the overall trend will objectively pave the way for new stabilization attempts at the end of the year.

Summing up, one must say that the general direction of Russian reform is sound enough and has virtually no alternative. The outcome of Russia's social and economic evolution will henceforth be determined not so much by what the state is doing but by the heavy burden of problems that are too much for the present government, and my the economy's capacity for self-organization and self-regulation.

WAS IT RIGHT TO LIBERALIZE THE PRICES FOR ENERGY RESOURCES?

Vladimir Kosenko, Cand.Sc.(Econ.)

FREEING THE PRICES FOR ENERGY RESOURCES: AN INCENTIVE OR A COUNTER-INCENTIVE?

The policy of Russia's government in the sphere of further price liberalization, including the prices for bread, milk, and energy resources, the introduction of internal currency convertibility on the basis of a fixed exchange rate of the rouble, and encouraging freer foreign-trade activity by abolishing quotas and licenses, is in keeping with the recommendation of the International Monetary Fund, whose loans we intend to use to guarantee the internal convertibility of the rouble by creating (after Poland's example) our own stabilization fund. The government's expects that liberalization of the prices for oil and gas will encourage producers to increase output (energy resources account for close to a half of all budget revenues).

However, the situation is not as simple as it may seem at first sight.

First, the sharp increase of prices for energy resources (for oil, from 350 roubles to 2000-2500 roubles per ton) is more likely to serve as a counter-incentive and not as an incentive, as was the case after price liberalization other industries.

Second, in 1991, Russia mined 11% less of oil than in 1990, thus losing 10 billion foreign currency equivalent roubles. In 1992, the drop in oil extraction was even greater, which can be explained by a number of reasons: the wear and tear and obsolescence of the equipment; the use of outdated technologies which only allow to extract not more than one-fourth of the actual amount of oil in the beds; and the outflow of qualified Azerbaijani and Ukrainian personnel. It is therefore doubtful that price liberalization alone can increase the production of energy resources, whereas the catastrophic consequences of this step are apparent.

Our economy has a unique quality, which no other economy in the world possesses: our wealth is the cause of our poverty. Everyone is aware that for a long time we have been able to make both ends meet only by selling our natural resources. But this is pure speculation, while what we need is a basis for our strategy of economic change. What does this mean?

We have entered an extremely painful stage of integration into the world economic system. And it has immediately become apparent that the more effort we put in into processing natural materials, the less competitive they become. Given the existing technical and technological level of our manufacturing industry and the quality of labor, it would pay not to process raw materials but to sell them in the world market. What conclusions can be made in regard to our today's practice?

The recommendations of the International Monetary Fund, which the government of Russia is following right now, are indisputable from the point of view of production efficiency. It is true that by the standards of industrialized countries, our manufacturing industry is only wasting our natural resources. In its present state it is absolutely useless. But then we have to recognize that roughly a half of Russia's population, which is employed in this industry, is also "useless".

When all prices for all goods are liberalized, when a convertible national currency is introduced, and when full-scale liberalization of foreign trade is carried out, it is only natural that, in line with the laws of a free market, all the resources will go where they shall be used most efficiently, i.e., abroad.

The government is planning to add another 30-35 million tons of oil to the already existing export quota of 60 million tons at the cost of lower consumption of energy resources after the prices for them have been freed. This additional amount can be easily doubled or even trebled, since the liberalization of prices for oil, gas and their side-products will inevitably result in a paralysis - a full stoppage of at least one-third of the manufacturing enterprises, because they will not be able to sell their products and, consequently, will not need the energy resources for their production.

According to the data provided by the State Committee for Price Formation, as a result of price liberalization, the prices for fuel (as compared to March) will rise more than four times, for ferrous metals - twice, machine-building products - almost twice, light industry products - more than twice, food - 1.6 times. Who will be able to buy a Zhiguli car for 500,000-600,000 roubles? It will cost 20,000-25,000 roubles to change a tyre. A Don combine harvester will cost over 17 million roubles. In addition, 20-30 million people will lose their jobs and will be unable to buy a loaf of bread for 10 roubles and a carton of milk at the same price. That is why we can only hope that the government will revise its economic tactics.

ADJUSTMENTS IN THE PRICE FORMATION POLICY

What should these adjustments be like? First, the planned liberalization of prices for energy resources, bread, and milk should be given up completely. Of course, in the future, we will reach the world level of oil and gas prices, but this should be done carefully, along with re-equipping our industry and doing away with its disproportions. Second, prices for goods produced by non-state enterprises can and should be liberalized. As for the state sector of industry, certain regulation is necessary (maximum profitability, progressive taxation). But the main thing is that prices for goods produced by state enterprises can only be liberalized after a currency reform of the kind introduced by Ludwig Erhard.

However, the government persistently neglects all recommendations of a currency reform.

The government's course of making the ruble convertible is as erroneous and premature. A certain parallel can be drawn between this course and the liberalization of prices. Liberalization does away with the difference between state and commercial prices, while the convertibility of the rouble results in their levelling.

From the point of view of world prices 100 roubles for 1 kg of meat is a low, dumping price at an exchange rate of 110 roubles for 1 dollar, because, for example, in the United States 1 kg of beef costs $5-8. But one must bear in mind that the monthly average earnings of a hired employee in the United States amounts to 3,000 dollars. Therefore, the top level of our internal prices is directed towards infinity.

The Polish idea of establishing its own stabilization currency fund was regarded without due criticism while trying to provide the internal convertibility of the rouble. This is a faulty idea, since it provides for an artificial (and temporary - until the fund is spent) convertibility of the national currency, while the economy is unable to guarantee such high demands. Turning a national currency into a freely convertible one is not a financial problem, it is a problem of a drastic restructuring and improvement of the entire national economy and its solution calls for much time and effort.

The introduction of a foreign currency into circulation devaluates a weak currency even quicker than emission. If the population possesses, for example, 3 billion dollars, this equals to an additional emission of 330 billion roubles. In this case any improvement of the financial system is out of the question. That is why the use of foreign currency in domestic circulation should be prohibited immediately, as a prerequisite of the stabilization of the rouble's purchasing capacity. But this is not enough. It is also necessary to return, at least temporarily, to differentiated foreign currency exchange rates. There should be one for foreign tourists, another, and more favorable one, for investors and still another one for local producers purchasing raw materials abroad. This measure demands a state monopoly for all currency exchange operations. And only after we reach the lowest degree of our descend and slowly begin to ascend, only then it will be possible to carry out a gradual "sluice-gate" merge of the rouble's exchange rates, which will allow our economy to gently overcome its disproportions and to integrate into the world economy.

INFLATION AND CRISIS: THE WAY OUT

S. Amosov, Ph.D. (Econ.)
Institute of Economics,
Russian Academy of Sciences

No country in the world has ever been able to avoid inflation and economic crises. But even the most gravest crises had resulted, as a rule, in a renewal and an upsurge of the economy. The means which helped other countries cope with crisis and overcome inflation must, probably, be applied in a somewhat different way in our particular situation. However, a country's own way must be based on a practically-tested theory and means already tested by other countries.

With the formation of markets of commodities, capital and labor, the scientific and technological and socioeconomic evolution began to be regularly interrupted by crises caused by a disturbance of reproduction and intra-branch proportions. In this case inflation was conditioned by a slowdown of the growth rate of the consumer sphere as compared to the investment sphere and by singular disproportions, influencing the money-commodity balance. In the course of over 100 years economic literature has been discussing the question of the presence or absence of a cycled reproduction in which the theories on the existence of middle-term and long-term cycles prevail.

Money-commodity disbalance and a disproportion in the development of industrial branches have always been typical of our economy. But a lack of markets of commodities, money and labor in combination with a centralized directive management of the economy gave rise to other forms of economic development, different from middle-term cycles and overproduction crises. A long-term cycle or a long wave are connected with the distribution of scientific and technological and socioeconomic progress from certain major industrial branches to others. Thus, the cycle brought about by the industrialization of social production has begun in our country prior to the revolution, but has not yet been completed. But the usual disproportions of the long-term cycle do not cause inflation and crises on such a large scale as at present. The stage through which Russia is going through nowadays possesses all the typical features of a ruin of the economy and state as a result of war and the present-day crisis can be viewed as a post-war crisis.

War crises differ from cycle crises by a more open and strong disproportion in favor of war supplies and by an obvious source of inflation in the form of government emission for covering defense spending. The scope of the destruction of the country's monetary system during the past several years can only be compared with the period of World War I, when in the course of 3 years, including 1917 the currency circulation in Russia increased by 14 times. This was enough for the state to collapse. During World War II the money circulation increased by 3.8 times.

During 1961-1991 the money supply in circulation increased by 37 times which is close to that of World War I. During 1986-1991 the money supply in circulation grew by 3.6 times, while in 1991 alone it almost doubled. This means that during the period of 1986-1991 the rate of inflation emission was approximately the same as during World War II (taking into account that the mass of commodities first grew insignificantly and then decreased altogether). However, in regard to the level of the monetary system's destruction the present crisis corresponds, to a greater degree, to the situation of 1917. At the same time, in regard to the scope of structural disproportions the present crisis corresponds, to a greater degree, to the crisis that took place after the war of 1941-1945. Russia entered World War I having a market economy, which made it possible to overcome the crisis during the period of the New Economic Policy by a quick restoration of market structures.

The post-war crisis that followed World War II was done away with in non-market conditions. Commodity and money circulation was revived in a strictly regulated form with an exclusion from commodity-monetary circulation of collective agricultural production and of a number of other spheres. Drastic measures were taken to stabilize the rouble. Firstly, a non-deficit budget was formed. After the introduction of energetic measures directed towards ensuring the production of goods and a number of other preparation measures a currency reform was carried out in 1947 during which cash was exchanged 10:1 with a much less confiscation of money on bank accounts. As a result, inflation was curbed, given the stable economic and political situation of those days. Defense enterprises were converted during the shortest possible period of time and were quite effective. By 1950 the country was able to double the output of the machine-building industry as compared to 1940. However, due to the non-market character of the economy, the defense structure of the national economy was preserved, despite conversion. During the period of post-war restoration the growth rate of the manufacture of means of production was twice as much as the manufacture of consumer goods. Simultaneously, tremendous resources were channelled to the military build-up. From the point of view of the resources consumption the war was still going on.

Therefore, the disproportions that existed in the economy during the war were preserved, which led to a crisis after the defeat in the "cold war". The battles in this war were purely of an economic nature. For example, the means spent in 1960-1970 for reinforcing the Soviet-Chinese border could have solved the problem of automobile roads throughout the entire country. Half of the means spent in the war in Afghanistan would have been enough to create a modern commodity-transportation network which would exclude loses of agricultural products. Half of the annual spending for supporting Castro's regime would have been enough to completely re-equip the domestic sugar-producing industry. One third of the means spent for the military exploration of the outer space would have been enough to telephonize and computerize all rural enterprises producing agricultural products 10-15 years ago. A conversion of only one plant putting out out-dated war machines would have fulfilled the demand of the manufacturing enterprises for modern technologies and equipment. The country had been defeated in all these instances.

An important feature of today's crisis is that for a long time it had been suppressed by the centralized directive system of management and at the cost of the intensive exploitation of natural and labor resources, the export of raw materials, administrative price rises, emission financing, etc. By 1989-1991 these means of preserving the extra-economic pressure on the national economy were completely exhausted. Attempts to solve the problem by restructuring the commanding-administrative system of management lead to the severance of economic ties and the replacement of state monopoly by corporative, bureaucratic and criminal monopoly. In these conditions the crisis of a post-war type has become an open-type crisis.

A diagnosis of the crisis allows to predict, with a 100% probability, the scenario of its evolution and the ways and means of coping with it. Both ours and foreign experience prove that such a crisis cannot be overcome without a radical limitation of war spending, decisive conversion and the formation of a non-deficit budget. There were some alternatives in world history in regard to a monetary reform and the liberalization of prices. Germany and Russia carried out post-war monetary reforms, while Japan and Italy did not. The refusal to carry out a monetary reform brought these countries to hyperinflation which had lowered the rate of national currencies for decades. Therefore, the only choice is between a monetary reform and hyperinflation.

Our low level of economic culture does not allow us to defeat the crisis with purely German pedantry. Nevertheless, even with greater expenses, we can only cope with this crisis by using the same means as post-war West Germany. Its experience differed from ours of the period of 1946-1950: it liquidated the monopoly structures in the military and industrial complex, carried out a more extensive conversion of the defense industry, cut down its defense expenses and embarked on a market economy. Conversion of the war industry and the structural reshaping of the economy in favor of the consumer sector were achieved in the course of two-three years on the basis of a combination of a state investment policy and free enterprise. It must be noted that military spending were cut down immediately, which made it possible to form a non-deficit budget. The structural reshaping was carried out along with legislative and bank stimulating of the formation of a competitive environment and economic expansion (boosting the manufacture of commodities). The liquidation of the budget deficit together with a monetary reform allowed to stabilize currency circulation.

The preparation for the liberalization of prices and incomes was completed by a commodity intervention with the help of American assistance. Prices and the population incomes were liberalized at the final stage of beating the crisis - in 1948. As a result, the growth of prices and wages during their liberalization was followed by a rapid growth of commodity production. A combination of a non-deficit budget, an orderly currency circulation, the growth of production with commodity intervention made it possible to avoid hyperinflation during price liberalization. The transition to a market economy was not followed by a drop in the standard of living but, on the contrary, took place against a background of a smoothing out of society's social differentiation. It provided for the growth of the purchasing capacity of all strata of the population. In this German experiences differs from our present-day inflationary accumulation of capitals by speculative means.

All attempts to use economic levers in our monopolistic economy only destroyed the budget, the finance and monetary systems which were not intended for market relations. The point is that the basic market economic lever - bankruptcy of ineffective producers - could not be used in a monopolistic economy. After that various anti-crisis programs directed towards changing property relations were considered. But a reshaping of the types of property can only be effective in a combination with the above-mentioned measures taken by Germany.

It must be noted that the attempts to get rid of the crisis by "sacrificing" the land to those who wish to take it are absolutely groundless. First, to run a farm its owner must possess the necessary qualifications. That is why in countries with developed agricultural production even the heirs do not have a right to receive the land free-of-charge, and for persons without a corresponding education and adequate means farming is out of the question altogether. Second, Polish experience shows that private ownership in agriculture cannot serve as a guarantee against recession in this sphere, given the clumsy, monopolistic structure of the national economy. And, finally, our own example of coping with the post-war crisis in the 1920s proves that a boost in trade between rural and urban regions began not after the announcement of the New Economic Policy, but in 1922, after the reduction of the number of troops and ended together with the procurements' crisis in 1926-1927, after the country entered a new turn in the militarization of the economy under the banner of intensified industrialization and preparation for a war with the surrounding capitalist countries.

Attempts to change the type of state property and privatize property in agriculture are aimed at cutting budget spending not by removing the extra-economic pressure on the national economy, but at the cost of reducing the state support of agriculture and the subsidizing of prices for food stuffs. Such an approach brings about hyperinflation. Only in November 1991 had the EEC countries adopted a decision to reduce state interference in the formation of prices on the agricultural market. Up to then, in the course of a long period of time, subsidies to farmers, for example, in the FRG, approximately equalled to the cost of the net products they produced. This goes to show that in conditions of a private ownership of land agriculture functions effectively if it is supported by society, and is not only a source of means used for state needs.

State support of agriculture, as well as containing prices for food are the two most important anti-inflation and anti-crisis measures. The demand for food stuffs is not flexible in regard to prices and that is why despite the liberalization of prices for agricultural products they may still remain very high. The growth of prices for food, bearing in mind the large share of the population's incomes spent on it, leads to an increase of incomes backed only by inflationary emission. Hyperinflation comes into the picture when, in a situation of a recession in production, a free growth of food prices is allowed. That is why the approach towards privatization in agriculture as towards an anti-crisis means is not justified without a solution of such issues as a non-deficit budget, conversion of the defense industry, structural reshaping, liquidity of money, etc.

This, of course, does not mean that property relations in agriculture should remain unchanged. But they must be modified along with the appearance of competitive commodities in all branches of the economy, including the military and industrial complex. But one must bear in mind that after agriculture is ridded of state property in any form, its commodity capacity will inevitable decrease in conditions of crisis and inflation. If land will be distributed without a persistent overcoming of the post-war type of crisis, the only way to solve the problem of food supplies would be to confiscate agricultural products from the producers with the help of military detachments as was the case in Russia in the 1920s.

The liberalization of prices and wages can lead, in principle, to a decrease of military spending, since during accelerated inflation budget allocations devaluate rapidly. According to data provided by the USSR Supreme Soviet Chamber of Control, at an annual inflation in 1991 of about 650-700% prices for goods necessary for maintaining the army grew at the same rate. But the division of the army and the interior troops between the independent republics, the re-stationing and not the reduction of troops that are pulling out of the countries of the former Warsaw Treaty and of the Baltic republics will result in the fact that the CIS republics will be compelled to resort to emission for covering military spending to a still greater degree than the Center. In other words, without an effective conversion of the war industry and the reduction of military spending we may be faced by a situation similar to that of 1917 when the "war for the Dardanelles till final victory" ruined the country's monetary system and wrecked both the army and the democratic government.

If we do not want the liberalization of prices and wages to cause hyperinflation, we must follow the example of post-war Germany. According to some opinions in the press, since such countries as the United States, Germany and Japan have a budget deficit, there is no use trying to create a non-deficit budget. Indeed, a budget deficit may be linked with the state's financing of extra-economic pressure on the national economy. Western experts hold that a market economy with a well-developed monetary circulation is able to sustain a 5% budget deficit connected with emission financing of social programs, education, culture, management, army, etc.

Liberalization of prices and incomes will be followed by moderate inflation during an expansion of commodity supplies, but not during a reduction of the commodity mass. In this connection we may ask: has a competitive environment for the liberalization of prices been created? Do the necessary conditions for the transfusion of capital to the production of products in high demand exist? What role will conversion play in establishing a market economy? The liberalization of prices in a market economy does not mean any kind of freedom in price formation, but only a freedom that ensures competition between producers, retail and wholesale structures. The assumption that speculation does not exist under conditions of a market economy, are unfounded. In all countries with a market economy there exist anti-monopoly or direct anti-speculation laws which prohibit speculation that damages the manufacturer by monopolistic rise of prices. These laws apply to all market institutions. For example, jobbers at agricultural stock markets in the Unites States are not allowed to occupy positions of brokers, for they play on the fluctuations of contract prices and thus, cannot be let to form these prices. Moreover, brokers at the US stock markets are not entitled to an interest from the sum of the deal, so as not to be interested in increasing the price.

The domination of state supplies in our country gave rise to such economic relations which function along the principles of classical monopoly. This system lacks all incentives for floating capital with the aim of checking deficit. A competitive environment must be created on the basis of an all-round promotion of entrepreneurship. However entrepreneurship in our country is still at the stage of the initial accumulation of financial capital and of nonproductive property. Through inflationary means the market structured have already amassed billions of roubles, but this process cannot continue forever. Either the inflationary commercial capital will start being actively invested into the manufacture of goods in demand, or hyperinflation will set in and the relative commodity deficit will turn into an absolute one.

The establishment of commodity markets is linked with a transition from state-monopoly structures to competitive ones. Today not a single state branch of industry is responsible economically for the fulfillment of the goods' demand. For example, despite the existing shortage in food stuffs, not a single link in the chain: grain growing - yielding - storing - processing - is not responsible for satisfying the demand for grain and grain products. In our agriculture an enterprise does not go bankrupt if it fails to harvest the whole crop. The grain elevators collect more profits from machinations with grain categories that from actually preserving the grain. The aim of the state mixed fodder industry was not to increase the productiveness of cattle-breeding, but to pump into the state budget means received at the cost of the difference in prices for grain and mixed fodder. In industrial production the situation is worsened by the sad fact that most of the factories do not work for the needs of the market, they put out goods which profitable to produce, but are ineffective or even useless. Monopolistic relations are also typical of the power industry, transportation, communications, construction and the circulation sphere. In order to get rid of this universal monopoly its primary source - state interference into the economy - must be done away with at once. The first thing to be done is to drastically cut the military orders which permeate the entire national economy through intra-branch ties and which, besides wasting resources, serve as the underlying reason of monopolistic relations.

The effect of cutting military spending and furthering the conversion of the defense industry is much greater than solving the budget problems and increasing the goods' supplies. A program of restructuring the war economy into a market economy can become a basis for national revival that would unite the people around the idea of creating a society of free citizens engaged in efficient business activity in market conditions. Anyhow, all attempts to form a competitive environment in the national economy without liquidating the monopoly of the military and industrial complex are doomed to failure.

The conversion of large military plants needs time. In some cases this time is needed to transfer from the production of singular items or small and middle series of products to the production of mass series. In other cases the assortment of articles supplied by other plants will have to be changed. Sometimes the specialized equipment becomes useless and has to be replaced. Despite all these factors, the effect from conversion could become noticeable even before it will be completed. First, this will be an effect from the demonopolization of the economy, of which we spoke above. Second, this will a multiple effect in saving and redistributing resources to civil spheres of the economy. Third, the military and industrial complex is capable of providing the national economy with certain products without conversion.

Conversion calls for large investments, the same as the reduction of troops demands considerable allocations for providing the former servicemen with housing, jobs, etc. The question here is from what sources will conversion and the military reform be financed. Budget financing in this case is inexpedient for the following reasons. It will not help check the budget deficit. There is no guarantee that the allocated budget means will be spent for conversion and not for the production of purposeless armaments. The experience of a budget financing of conversion in 1989-1991 has proved the futility of such an approach. The problems shall be solved when conversion will be financed by the free capitals of non-state of organizations and also by foreign investors. This will be a solution of a whole knot of problems: budget deficit, inflation, entrepreneurship, investments, conversion and market development. This would be the best way out of the crisis.

INFLATION IN RUSSIA'S ECONOMY: ORIGINS AND TENDENCIES

P. Lushin, Ph.D.(Econ.),
Director of the Finance Research Institute

V. Pashkovsky, Ph.D (Economy),
Department Head of the Finance Research Institute

The transition from a directive economy to market relations has essentially increased the significance of money. Money circulation is the basic issue of both practical measures intended for remodelling the national economy and theoretical research. That is why, despite the lively discussions of these question in economic newspapers and publications, they remain as urgent as always. The working out of an optimum monetary policy is hampered by the difficulty in analyzing the inflationary processes and by the presence of a large number of active factors.

As it has been proven by the experience of our and other countries, the transition to market economic relations is followed by a rapid growth of prices and by an intensification of inflationary factors. To this end, it is important to determine whether the transition to market relations per se is the reason of enhanced inflation or these relations have unleashed the previously accumulated inflationary potential.

The experience of many countries has shown that long periods of centralized economic planning cause, as a rule, a disproportion in the material and currency spheres. In regard to Russia this was expressed in a deformation of the national economy structure and in an excessive production of means of production in the country's total industrial output. The intense methods of economic development resulted in an intolerable investment burden, in the freezing of tremendous resources in the excessive production funds, in numerous incomplete construction projects and exorbitant material stocks. One must bear in mind that for the production and the subsequent "freezing" of all these material values salaries had been paid, as well as bonuses for good work and work incentive funds were set up. In recent years the disproportion between commodities and money was enhanced because of the increasing sums of budgetary subsidies which, in turn, increased the incomes of both industrial enterprises and the population. No material values back these growing incomes in a framework of administrative planning. If we add to this the "parity" defense expenditures and the fulfillment of the population's needs by the remaining means we will get a more or less full picture. The disproportion of our economy is generally expressed in the three following indicators: the deficit of the state budget, the accumulation of hopeless debts to the bank on the part of economic organizations and the prevalence of the population's incomes over their spending. It is obvious that the country's structure of production and distribution gave rise to various disproportions and, firstly, to an excess of incomes as compared with the material resources.

It must be noted that disproportion in the economy per se do not necessarily disturb the material-financial balance. Theoretically, such a balance can be maintained under any disproportions at the cost of rising prices and limiting the population's incomes. But such a policy has a certain risk from the social point of view and depends on the sternness of the decisions adopted by the directing center. In the classical sense centralized planning existed in our country only until 1965. The period from 1950 to 1964 can be considered as a relatively favorable one for the financial and material balance which was attained mostly at the cost of a strict limitation of the income growth and price maneuvering. In the course of the reform, which began in 1965, certain compromises were made in the sphere of forming the population's incomes. These included the establishment of material incentive funds at enterprises, paying one additional monthly salary in the end of the year and regular increases of labor remuneration in certain branches and regions, as well as in the entire economy, mostly at the cost of budgetary means. Thus, the growth of incomes took place independently, without any progress in labor efficiency, resources saving and in the production of new goods. The incomes of the population grew simply because such a grow had been planned and its actual rates almost always exceeded the planned ones. This process gained momentum during the 1970s. Thus the foundation was laid of the present inflation and the universal conviction that the incomes can be and should be increased.

At the beginning of perestroika the enterprises became more independent and thus relieved themselves of the last administrative limitations of the growth of the personnel's incomes (a fixed wage fund, a correlation between the growth of labor efficiency and the average salaries, etc.). The attempt to establish a tax regulating the growth of the wage fund was, in essence, brought to nil, by the numerous amendments to the corresponding law. The population's incomes grew in 1989 by 12.9%, in 1990 - by 17.0% and in 1991 - by 87%.

The expansion of disproportions is favored by the existing structure of industrial production, the prolonged priority development of enterprises of the "A" group, characterized by a high labor intensiveness and excessive remuneration. Therefore, the growth of wages sharply surpasses the manufacture of consumer goods.

The aggravation of the inflation situation is connected with the absolute drop in the volume of production which began in 1990 and which by 1991 acquired a scope typical of that of a crisis. Despite the traditions and laws of a market economy, the drop in the rate of production in this case was not accompanied by a reduction of the enterprises and population's incomes. A self-maintaining process of constantly increasing monetary incomes of all types has set it. It is independent of the actual dynamics of material production and is distinguished by a growing budget deficit and price rise. Such a process seems to be an inevitable consequences of the structural break down of the economy and of the price and income systems. All faults and disproportion which had accumulated during the years of stagnation must be removed, but this will be connected with losses and with a reduction of the enterprises and population's incomes. The inevitable losses and damages are formed not like direct deductions from incomes, but as a result of differences in the comparative dynamics of prices and incomes of various legal and physical entities. Inflation plays the role of a payment for the structural reshaping of the entire economic system in the course of advancing towards a market economy and, at the same time, the role of a means of this advance. In the odd socio-psychological atmosphere that exist presently in Russia, which is trying to shift from centralized planning of the economy to a classical market economy there appears a situation unfamiliar to normal market relations, when price and commodity shortage grow simultaneously.

FACTORS AND PROSPECTS OF INFLATIONARY PROCESSES

The full liberalization of prices calls for the adoption of certain decisions in the sphere of the population's incomes: either removing all income limitations or their regulation with various degrees of strictness. An instant elimination of control over prices and incomes and the introduction of an indexation of the latter will, more likely, result in a many-zero and prolonged inflation that will block economic development, since it undermines the determination to investment, to the development and improvement of production. Drawn-out inflation is always followed by a tremendous upsurge of speculation on price changes, which lowers the employees' incentives for conscientious labor.

The forecasts of the possible price changes during their liberalization often proceed from the normative calculations of the coming increase of incomes. And since the growth of incomes is limited (in the calculations) a conclusion is made on the limitation of price growth. In other words, the limitation of the price growth is concluded from a limitation of the solvent demand. But the fault of this assumption lies in the fact that it does not take into account the fact that the growth of prices causes a growth of incomes. Thus appears a dangerous process with positive reverse feedback. Large-scale estimations on a "national economy" level are in general of little significance. The price, which is a very concrete showing, depends on the particular conditions of the production and sale of a given commodity. A considerable price rise for one product is enough to cause a jump of incomes which has not been specified by any calculations. As a result, the demand for other goods will also grow and this, in turn, will set off a multiplicator of incomes, demand and price increase. The probability of such events on a monopolized market, and our coming market will be such, is very high. Russia's policy in the sphere of the liberalization of wages and prices threatens to cause a drawn out and large-scale inflation. Such a policy can only be successful if the budget deficit is curtailed drastically and the granting of bank loans is strictly controlled. It is also necessary to regulate the incomes and prices, so as not to delay the process of attaining a balance and to reach a social compromise. For example, a price court of arbitration may be established, which would consider the customers' objections to high prices; state recommendations during signing collective contracts could be made, etc.

If the prices and wages are merely "set free" and indexation is only limited to pensions and social benefits of a minimum size, the balance can be obtained quickly, due to an accelerated price growth. In the free race of prices and wages the prices will always be the winner, since inflationary expectations devaluate money (incomes) and make the consumers prefer commodities. "Running away from money" leads to a stable prevalence of demand over supply and favors a more rapid growth of prices. But a market balance achieved in such a way will most likely be of an extreme nature, i.e., the level of prices will be the maximum, the real incomes of the population will drop as will the volume of production. Society's expenditures for such a balance in the economy will be too high. It is much better to find the mean middle, to reach a state of balance in the course of the shortest possible period and with a minimum of losses in real incomes and in the volume of production and also at a moderate rate of inflation. An optimum combination of these contradictory factors cannot be achieved without external interference into the dynamics of prices and wages. That is why of such importance during a period of inflation are a taxation policy, a firm checking of the budget deficit, the interest level and dynamics, a credit policy, the savings rate and insurance.

The indexation of incomes plays a special role here, since the rate of inflation during liberalized prices and incomes in many ways depends on the size of the wage indexation. There is no clear theory concerning this, but by purely empirical means there has been determined a maximum admissible correlation between the price growth rate and wage indexation during which inflation ceases to grow: 0.2, i.e., it is best not to index incomes more than by 1/5 of the price growth rate.

Income indexation should be applied very carefully and only for the population in the low-income bracket, otherwise the growth of incomes will disturb the market balance.

The influence of the incomes' dynamics on inflation does not exclude a certain state control of the price level. This is especially important for our economy. The possibilities of state control of price forming under market conditions have hardly been studied in our country. We still have to master a whole complex of measures which are applied in other countries on a broad scale. These include a direct limitation of prices for certain types of goods, a system of taxation measures, the creation of a competitive milieu, the establishment of new relations with the consumers, including local authorities and consumer societies, etc. All these measures are introduced on a legal basis with a serious material responsibility.

A transition to marker relations radically changes the role of the financial and credit policy in economic life and increases its influence on the current economic processes. New possibilities appear. Of special interest here are the changes of taxes and depreciation rates and loan interests-- this is much easier to carry out that, for example, decreasing the budget deficit or reviewing the exchange rate of the rouble.

Increasing taxes is itself a very adverse factor, since it can result in a drop of production efficiency after the enterprise or entrepreneur are left with a small amount of free means and since it reduces the tax-payers' incentives for business activity. Such an evaluation of a tax increase is independent of inflation.

If there do not exist any administrative limitations of the price growth, and they should not exist in conditions of a real market, in this case the influence of taxes (their increase) depends on whether each entrepreneur (enterprise) is able to compensate the tax increase by a price rise, i.e., whether the market will accept the increased prices. If yes, then the tax growth itself will become an inflationary factor. The greater the tax growth rate, the higher the prices. But this cannot go on forever. There can be tax rates which demand for their compensation such prices which are inadmissible for the market. Besides, there can be another outcome of the tax increase, when the manufacturer losses interest in expanding production and even stabilizing it, no matter the size of the price for his products. In other words, even if the increased tax may be compensated by an increase of prices, its sum is so large, that the producer is no longer interested in his business.

If the market does not allow increasing the price, the producer is left with less means at his disposal. Whether he will be able to compensate the absolute reduction of means depends on the dynamics of the mass of the products to be sold. But, obviously, in this case the increase of taxes will "suppress" production. That is why in conditions of a "normal" market a tax increased is followed by either a rise in prices or by a worsening of the manufacturer's economic situation. Although the latter contains certain anti-inflation moments (due to a drop of the manufacturers' demand), in general it obstructs economic development.

In addition, the state, having received extra monetary resources, will direct them towards fulfilling its own needs, which will lead to an increased demand in other spheres of the economy. The aggregate demand in society will remain unchanged, while the change in its structure may affect the price growth in other spheres of the economy. This also undermines the anti-inflation effect of the tax increase.

Therefore, the anti-inflation role of a tax increase is only possible under quite harsh prerequisites and in quite a narrow framework. On the one hand, it presumes a decrease of the enterprise's financial resources, i.e., a decrease in the demand of the income owners, but, on the other, it must not be followed by a compensating or an outstripping price growth and by a loss of motives for business activity and a subsequent drop of production. It is quite difficult to keep to such contradictory conditions.

The period of transition from an administrative economy to a market economy is characterized by a number of specific traits. Among them is the fact that the monopolistic enterprises of the state sector view their growing independence as a means of increasing prices for their products and thus, paying higher wages to their personnel. An attempt to level the incomes of various social strata of the working population by increasing them is one of the primary factors of inflation nowadays. Can a change of the taxation system in this situation suppress the growth of prices and, consequently, the incomes? This implies both taxes on profits (or total income) and taxes on employees' incomes (the general wage fund and personal incomes). The tax on profits, which is regarded as an anti-inflation measure, must have as its object part of the profits derived from the price increase. An extraction of this part of the profits makes the price growth useless for the producer. It is important to establish more than one tax on profits: one or two, of which the first is on "usual" profits and the second on super profits derived from the price increase. It seems more expedient to have two taxes, since the tax on super profits is in a sense an extraordinary and somewhat temporary tax, which serves as a means of checking inflation. In this case there should be a special object for the tax on super profits. In general it may be the difference between the volume of production in permanent and current prices. But this is a very stern approach. Since a transition to a market economy provides for the introduction of free prices, a certain price growth should be allowed. Everything that exceeds it must be turned over to the budget in the form of a tax on super profits.

During such a model of anti-inflation taxation, the dynamics of the volume of production in permanent prices becomes the basic indicator. Working out a corresponding index to be applied to enterprises shall serve as a guarantee of the tax's effectiveness. In the practical sense certain exemptions are possible in regard to this tax. Not all super profits may be appropriated, but only 75-90%; for certain products higher prices may be allowed, etc. The anti-inflation effect of taxation at the same time provides for a checking of prices and incomes.

Individual taxation of citizens, when it is based on the progressive principle, is itself an anti-inflation measures, since in this case the growth of incomes leads to an increase of the average tax rate. Here special anti-inflation measures may not be introduced, it is enough to introduce a progressive tax scale.

The taxation of the general wage fund at enterprises (firms) is also of an anti-inflation nature, but the same as during taxation of profits certain conditions must be observed and the prices growth must not be stimulated.

Under conditions of a transition to a market economy taxes may serve as an effective anti-inflation means only within the framework of all similar measures, and, firstly, price and credit measures.

A financial anti-inflation policy must be accompanied by an anti-inflation credit policy. There are various means of credit anti-inflation regulation. The level and dynamics of interest on the banks' passive and active operations are of primary importance. The interest rate actually indicates the "price" of the money during its transference from one owner to another for temporary use. The interest encourages two important economic processes: saving money by the population and enterprises (including long-term saving) and the active use of money in production with the aim of making a profit and also returning loans and paying interest to the owner of the money.

It is believed that increasing the interest rate is a necessary and universal means of slowing down inflationary processes. A high interest rate on loans lowers the demand for money and, consequently, the solvent demand for commodities. A reduction of demand stabilizes prices and contains their growth. The increase of the interest rate also creates greater incentives for saving money and in such a way reduces the current demand of both consumers and production. This kind of a policy is pursued by our banks.

As a rule, a country's interest policy is coordinated by the establishment, by the Central Bank, of a discount rate which serves as a foundation for all other banks. This is a soft market mechanism of guiding the mass of currency.

If an economy is characterized by a stable price growth, the monetary savings of all subjects of the economy and the received loans will be devaluated. With the aim of protecting their economic interests the banks are compelled to take into account the inflationary component while establishing the size of the interest, i.e., there appears a difference between the real and nominal interest. A prolonged maintenance of high interest in itself becomes an inflationary factor. Hence the anti-inflation influence of interest growth is only effective at the early stages of inflation, whereas when it is measured by two-digit numbers (as well as the interest), this influence becomes quite insignificant. This gives rise to a reciprocal influence -- of the interest growth on the price rate and the price growth on the interest rate. The high level and further growth of interest rates is capable of hampering the development of production, which enhances inflationary processes. That is why the general rise of the price of loans as a means of creating expensive money must be gently combined with the introduction of loan privileges for certain branches of the national economy which will make it possible to expand the production of consumer goods and, thus, steady the currency circulation.

A control over the general mass of currency in the national economy allows to most fully determine the possibilities and tendencies of influencing inflationary processes. This is a new approach to the monetary-credit policy which is yet to be comprehended. Regulating the general mass of currency makes it possible to determine the whole complex of factors influencing the currency stability.

An extremely negative practice of crediting has taken shape in recent years, when along with a considerable reduction of loans to the national economy, the number of loans directed towards fulfilling budgetary needs is growing constantly. Moreover, the bulk of loans to the national economy is used for solving various financial problems,

A lack of mediators (with their own economic interests) between the budget and loans in the form of a financial market causes a situation when all the factors of the budget deficit growth directly influence crediting and, consequently, inflationary processes. At present the credit system in Russia is not only unable to curb inflation, but only enhances it.

Such a loan orientation has deformed the credit resources. The currency means, which had been formed as a result of granting unjustified and unsecured loans, have been accumulated on the accounts of enterprises and the population, lacking any material equivalent and being a reflection of the economy's disproportions. These processes have distorted the content of various elements of the aggregate mass of currency. Even its most dynamic elements, such as cash and the means of enterprises cannot be used quickly enough to purchase necessary goods in view of the present-day shortages. Studies show that their circulation has slowed down considerably. They mirror the serious disproportions which are not easy to overcome in a short period of time. This calls for altered methods of analyzing the aggregate mass of currency and a new credit and financial policy as a means of influencing this mass.

In order to stabilize currency circulation it is necessary to change the structure of the aggregate mass of currency, to reduce the size and share of the most dynamic currency means. It is also important to provide a well-grounded correlation between money used for current consumption and long-term savings. Only after fulfilling its every-day needs will the population become interested in saving money and placing it in profitable sections of saving. And this calls for an active crediting of expenses connected with expanding the production of consumer goods. The establishment of commercial banks did not bring about a radical improvement in loan orientation. Commercial banks are interested in deriving maximum profits from crediting various mediatory commercial operations, thus intensifying the inflationary process.

There is a very close link between the development of state loans and the organization of the banking system. As a rule, in conditions of an underdeveloped banking system and meager bank resources, state loans take the shape of bonds and other securities distributed directly among the population and partially among enterprises. The creation of a diversified banking system, the accumulation by the banks of substantial resources and currency and the formation of a market of credit resources will enable the banks to invest their resources in the purchase of securities as well.

New inflationary problems will arise after the introduction of national currencies, which is inevitable because of the elimination of the centralized government which used to regulate the budgets of the republics. The formation of independent states with their own budgets facilitates the appearance of national currencies. The transition to a national currency is closely linked with the problem of dividing the internal state debt. Only in case the national currencies will be exchanged for the all-union currency at a rate 1:1 the republics will take upon themselves the full responsibility for paying off the state debt.

Russia: A Chance to Recover on the Basis of a Mixed Economy

Lev Nikiforov

In 1992 Russia entered a new stage in its development - the formation of an independent state, making its first step in the direction of a new social order. The old artificial and deadlock social system could not transform into a new by natural course. Its collapse did not predetermine a new system to replace it. Besides, while this system was disintegrating, the social situation in the country changed drastically. The various social strata and forces, both the old and newly-evolved, view the future of Russia proceeding from their own interests. As for the general tendencies which have taken shape in the course of privatization and the revival of a free market, they may have a different outcome, depending in keeping with whose interests they will be carried out. All this gives rise to various options in the country's future development.

This situation is aggravated by the fact that due to a erroneous strategy and tactics of the country's leadership which tried to alter and preserve the old oligarchic system, its break up caused economic chaos, a decrease of the rate of production, the drop in the people's standard of living and the destruction of the state. Whether the people and the country will survive has become the crucial problem of our time. The worsening of nationalities relations, the use of the growing national self-consciousness in political intrigues and in the struggle for power may lead to a tragedy for tens of millions of people divided by state principles, torn away from their peoples and involved in vain nationalities discord and confrontation.

Today it is much more difficult to introduce changes than in 1989, not only because of the severance of economic ties, the rapidly increasing resource shortage and the ruble devaluation, but because this anti-economic chaos is undermining production incentives, centering entrepreneurs around turnover speculation. This is where big capitals are made, which have nothing to do with the creation of either material or intellectual products.

In the existing conditions the attempts to use standard remedies for stabilizing the economy and overcoming the shortages turn out to be ineffective, because of the non-standard, from the point of view of world practice, situation of economic and state ruin. There is not such theory which would help work out a strategy for reforming the social system. The old theory of social development has gone bankrupt together with the social system which had been built on its basis. As a result, such vague ideas as "joining the flow of world civilization", "following the path of civilized countries", "creating a prospering society" are used as targets for the future change. But all these good intentions are not enough for setting the strategy and tactics of Russia's evolution.

In these circumstances the state power may decide to introduce the universal socioeconomic changes along administrative lines in response to the changes in the current situation. This pressure gives rise to resistance, thus making it impossible to create a prospering society. It is necessary to stop and think, to more clearly determine the aims and goals of the future changes and to view the first results of the reforms objectively, and not as the reformists would want to see them.

The Flow of World Civilization?

While determining the ways and means of changing the social system in Russia, one must take in account not only the collapse of the state oligarchic system per se, but those actual changes which both preceded it and took place after it in economic relations, the social structure of the society and its political and state composition. At the same time, it is necessary to grasp the essence of the socioeconomic transformations that are taking place in the developed countries and to pay attention to the changes in the conditions, factors and types of the people's productive activity, the ways and forms of their social organization.

The increasing role of the computer science, latest technologies, production and economic relationships and the other results of scientific and economic progress have greatly encouraged the people's social mobility. The more or less fixed borderlines between various social strata and groups are being erased. The existing class type of social differentiation is being gradually replaced by a more dynamic differentiation characterized by a different social and functional nature. The high-tech economy provides for the existence and competition of both large-scale and small production and various social types of businesses capable of effectively developing in all spheres of the economy.

On the whole, the social orientation and social dynamics create the necessary prerequisites for the social structures' mobility, the improvement of the standard of living of every social group and, on the whole, the full realization of the personality's potentials.

It is another thing that this potential is realized through contradictions, a struggle, the striving for accord and partnership of various social forces, interests, structures, and forms.

The social orientation of development makes one wish to achieve a maximum economic and social effect. And this is only possible at a combination of the economic structures and forms of different social types. Competing with each other and occupying those spheres in which each of them is more efficient than the others, these various structures and methods may provide for the greater general efficiency. In other words, the practical realization of the economy's social orientation excludes the monopoly of one social form. The historical arena is being entered by social formations based on a multitude of social forms, which are, in this sense, socially mixed or polyform. The systems of a polyform natures are typical not of a transitional stage in society's development (from one formation to another), but of a new type of civilization. This is the main tendency in the transformation of the modern capitalist society.

The dynamics of this type of state organization and the mobility of its socioeconomic and other public structures predetermine the versatility of the polyform systems. Precisely this circumstance is capable of guaranteeing the stability of mixed systems, their possibility to respond to the changing situations, development levels and other factors. The greater the number of options of this system's development, the more stable it is. There is no place here for a strict determination of economic relationships. For example, social orientation is a general line, to be more exact, a requirement of development. It is a result of the relationships and realization of many relations and it may be reached through their various concrete combinations and systems.

That is why a transition to such a type of systems excludes the possibility of creating them according to theoretical plans or models. At the same time, the formation of a polyform system presupposes the creation of certain conditions and a favorable economic, social and political environment.

The free dynamics of forms and relationships of property should stand out among these conditions. However, there is a number of features which must be typical of the majority of forms of property in the framework of polyform systems. These include: private principles in appropriating the means and results of business activity; an ability to adapt to the changing market conditions; efficiency necessary for the participation in solving social problems. This means that those forms of property will be most effective (from the point of view of satisfying the internal needs of a polyform society's development) which, in one way or another, ensure the position of individuals as private owners. The correlations of various forms of property must be based on their competitiveness, the level of economic and social efficiency of each of them.

The evolution of the polyform systems presupposes the creation of various political foundations. One of these is a transition from a political power of a dictatorship nature to a political democracy. Political democracy as a system of political power is characterized by at least three features:

- the possibility to change power in a lawful way in case it fails to satisfy the majority of the people;
- the isolation of political power from the economy and limiting the power's interference into the economy by adopting corresponding regulations, by the state's control over the fulfillment of these regulations by the economic structures; the fulfillment of state programs;
- the protection by the state of the interests of various social strata, i.e., the socially consolidating role of political power.

The beginning of the formation of the polyform systems in the developed countries was predetermined by the transition to high-tech stages of development which have created new conditions for the development and cooperation of large-scale and small production and business which, in turn, lead to both the increase of the general standard of living and the social mobility of various strata of the population. The appearance of a mixed economy is a natural result of the democratization of capital and other socioeconomic changes of a economy functioning in reliable market conditions with according regulating mechanisms. In addition, the basic democratic political prerequisites had been created.

Nevertheless, the evolution of polyform social systems, which has been unfolding for decades, has not yet been completed and is going through various stages and is taking different forms in different countries.

RUSSIA'S PATH

Thus, the tendency of the developed countries to become polyform, attests to the fact that this is a predetermined path of development. However, the situation in Russia makes a transition to such a form extremely difficult.

First, the oligarchic system failed to create such a high production and science and technological level which could serve as a basis for various types of economies in the present-day developed countries.

Second, the oligarchic system produced an exceedingly monopolistic state economy, which obstructs the development of a variety of socioeconomic forms and competition among them.

Third, the universal structural disproportions in the economy hinder its re-orientation towards the social interests and the needs of the people.

Fourth, as a result of the collapse of the oligarchic system and the subsequent changes in the social structure of society new social forces have appeared who are not always interested in progressing towards a mixed society.

Fifth, the very fact that the old party and state structures have been removed from power and done away with and that the power has been transferred to the new forces does not mean a transition from a dictatorship to democracy. Russia still lacks all the above-mentioned guarantees of democracy. Proof to this is the attempts of the new executive bodies to suppress the representative bodies under the pretext of an existing threat for democracy; in some cases the uncontrolled actions of the former under the pretense of introducing reforms or combatting the partocracy; the still existing subordination of the economy to the state power; the possibility to distribute state means in the interests of the structures of power or certain persons. The political power in Russia is at crossroads and may chose either democracy or dictatorship under the pressure of various factors.

All this not only creates difficulties for the transition to the most favorable polyform social system, but the requisites for other options of development.

The least possible of these is the revival of the wrecked oligarchic system, even in the form of "socialism with a human face", or something of the kind. The impossibility of restoring the old system opens a perspective of moving towards capitalism, or, rather, to its different versions. At present there have appeared social forces and strata interested in the establishment of monopolistic pseudo-entrepreneurship (due to their monopolistic nature) structures and in their domination in the economy. The establishment of such structures is facilitated by the high level of the economy's monopolization and by the opportunity to replace the former state departments by these structures. This is the goal of a part of the old state and party apparatus and of a certain part of the new power apparatus which used (and even surpassed) the process of the disintegration of state departments and their structural branches for founding various corporations, concerns and joint-stock companies, thus appropriating state means and resources.

This process can be justly called nomenclature privatization. The danger of such a monopolistic pseudo-capitalism lies in the fact that it not only fails to promote entrepreneurship and a free market but, on the contrary, due to its monopolistic nature, obstructs (especially in conditions of a resources shortage) the development of middle and small business, as well as large-scale entrepreneurship. The initial linkage between these structures with the former or present government representatives opens the way for corruption and mafia ties, for creating the most favorable conditions for the development of the structures they are "in charge" of. A limited number of persons is taking part in privatization (the participation of the broad masses is practically excluded) and many faults of the state oligarchic system are preserved and even reproduced in a modified and even in a more dangerous form. Such changes require a strong dictatorship also because they are fraught with a threat of an aggravation of tension and of a social explosion, because they are unable to provide solutions to the most urgent economic problems. They will cause a sharp property differentiation in society and will evoke the discontent of the broad masses, including the new strata of entrepreneurs. Due to the above-mentioned circumstances, this option cannot become the most perspective one.

Another option which has appeared recently is to introduce changes favoring the creation of a capitalist, free enterprise society. It is supported by, firstly, the evolving strata of small and middle business owners. However the development in this direction is impeded by the above-mentioned factors and, mainly, by the monopoly in the economy and the resources shortage. That is why the middle and small business turn into a kind of monopolistic structures usually dispersed formally, but which establish monopoly prices and limit or oust competitors, thus favoring the development of mafia relations and criminal incidents.

An example of this is the nature of the initial accumulation of capital, which is accomplished not simply at the cost of speculative turnover, but at the cost of a turnover in the sphere of circulation, at the cost of the appearance in it of a network of additional, often useless, links. A capital amassed in such a way is not directed towards production, the more so that it is not backed by material resources.

While evaluating on the chances and expedience of transforming the old social system along capitalist lines, the following factors must be taken into account. First, the state of the economy and society in general which ensures the appearance, to a great degree, of not entrepreneur, but pseudo-entrepreneur and thus pseudo-capitalist structures, which will make it harder to survive, to overcome the state of economic ruin and to advance production and entrepreneur activities.

Second, the increase of social tension in society is fraught with the threat of establishing a political dictatorship. Third, the influence on the orientation of Russia's socioeconomic changes of its world economic ties and the general tendencies of world progress, which will favor its progress not towards a capitalist society, but towards a post-capitalist, polyform society. It seems that in the end Russia will begin to create a new, mixed society.

Nowadays the idea on Russia's movement towards capitalism as something definite is wide-spread, including the structures of state power. The practical changes in accordance with this version are enhanced by the chosen methods of privatization which prevent the broad masses from taking part because of the delays in granting privatization voucher and because of the drop in the population's standard of living; by methods reforming price formation and not allowing to eliminate the speculative turnover and thus sharply decreasing the people's standard of living; by the taxation system which places most of the production structures, including those who are shifting to free enterprise, in a grave economic situation.

However, does Russia need another historical twist? Why not embark along the path leading to the creation of a modern post-capitalist society with practically unlimited perspectives and based on the cooperation and coordination of various economic, social and political forces and structures?

Undoubtedly, this is a complex road, but it is much more preferable than any other "simple" one. And if we have at least one chance out of a hundred we do not have the right to miss it. We do possess a foundations for the development of versatile socioeconomic types of business and an evolving market infrastructure necessary for their activity along the lines of entrepreneurship.

The chief advantage of this option lies in the fact that it opens wide vistas for the participation in the transformation of the old system to practically all strata of the population, which will help eliminate social confrontation and tension. This, in turn, will be a factor of changing to a democratic political power. Such a transition is possible, since the present political power has not yet turned into a power of strictly determined social forces and strata.

We can also make use of the work experience of various mixed systems. But, of course, in all cases the movement towards a post-capitalist society will not be easy, it will be resisted by the old and some new economic structures and social forces. The more so we need a well-elaborated strategy and tactics for reforming. But this is a theme of another publication.

CURRENCY AND FISCAL TREATMENT OF FOREIGN INVESTMENTS

S.M.Ryumin

The forms and conditions of the establishment of joint ventures and their financial and economic activities are regulated by a body of laws. The confidence of foreign investors can be built up by bilateral intergovernmental agreements on mutual encouragement and mutual protection of investments and prevention of double taxation of the incomes and property.

TAXATION OF FOREIGN INVESTMENTS

The profit tax for the joint ventures on the territory of the Russian Federation used to be 25% (30% in the other republics).

The joint ventures were tax exempt for the term of the first two years after the first declared profit (so-called "taxation holiday").

The joint ventures did not pay the turnover tax.

Preferential valuation of taxable profits as compared to those of native enterprises was permitted.

These rules remained unchanged for more than three years, but in 1990 the taxation system was revised.

"Taxation holidays" were given only to joint ventures operating in the sphere of material production and only during the first two years since the time of receipt of balance profit.

The taxation of joint ventures was differentiated depending on the branch in which they operated.

The part of the profits received over five years after losses have been reported and used to cover them was tax exempt.

The obligation to pay turnover tax was extended to the joint ventures; easier average taxation rates for individual goods were introduced.

Increased excess profits levy was introduced for the joint ventures (the reference is to the part of the profits over and above the top profitability level in the sector). However, the profitability ceiling above which the rate of the profit tax was sharply raised as compared to native enterprises was made twice as high (for all Russian enterprises whose profitability level exceeds the 50% maximum, the profits corresponding to this excess are taxed at the 75% rate).

However, these privileges extend to enterprises with foreign investments (with due account for the top profitability level) only if the latter's share constitutes more than 30% of registered capital.

JOINT VENTURES: RULES AND TERMS OF ESTABLISHMENT

Foreign investors may invest capital in Russia by: having a share in companies and enterprises together with Russian legal persons and individuals; setting up enterprises fully owned by foreign investors; purchasing property, including stock and other securities; purchasing the right to use land and other natural resources, as well as other property rights independently or with participation of legal persons or individuals; entering into contract with legal persons and citizens providing for other forms of foreign investment. At the moment, the prevalent form is joint ventures set up on share basis.

A foreign investor may set up a joint venture either together with other legal persons and/or individuals, or by buying a contribution (share, stock) in a previously established company without foreign investment. The law encourages foreign investors to contribute more than 30% to registered capital, in which case the company receives extensive financial and other privileges. Apart from the ones discussed above, such joint ventures do not need a license to export their own produce and to import goods for their own use. They may freely dispose of the convertible currency yielded by the export of their own produce, the restrictions imposed on the spending on labor remuneration do not extend to them, etc.

Legal Regulation of Registered Capital of Joint Ventures

Until lately the law did not specify either the minimum registered capital of companies with foreign participation, or the deadline by which the participants were to contribute their share of the capital (this could be done, in principle, at any time). The Law on Foreign Investments in the RSFSR has established control over this matter. If a year after registration a participant has failed to contribute to registered capital at least 50% of the sum named in the registration documents, the company is considered non-existent and is struck off the register of joint ventures. Companies with foreign investment in the form of joint ventures, limited liability companies, and any other type of company not contradicting the operating law may be set up. Under the Russian statutes, the nominal registered capital of a public joint-stock company may not be below 50,000, and of a private one - 10,000 roubles.

Analysis of the establishment and operation of joint ventures reveals the tendency towards setting up small enterprises in the industries that do not demand large investments and ensure the latter's quick recoupment (trade, public catering, etc.). Obviously, in this case the chief target is not attained, namely, attracting up-to-date technologies, equipment, and machinery, and the budget also suffers where it should not. I believe that minimum registered capital varying depending on the field of the joint venture's operation should be established. This practice is widely used in a number of countries to attract foreign investments.

The Profits of Foreign Investors

The fundamental law on foreign investment states that the profits of foreign investors may be reinvested. Virtually all ex-republics allow this. But Russia's Law draws a clear line between the forms of investment used on the country's territory: setting up a company jointly with legal persons and individuals, or purchasing a share in an already existing company, stocks, bonds, or other securities.

Chapter 3 of the RSFSR Law, "The Establishment and Abolition of Enterprises Using Foreign Investments", does not provide for special rules of their institution and operation for any particular form of the foreign investor's participation in registered capital, e.g., contribution of convertible or national currency. The need for uniform rules for investment into newly-established joint ventures stems from the very fact of their organization. The foreign partner is to supply them with up-to-date high-quality equipment and machinery, technologies, and know-how, and, as the experience of already working joint ventures shows, this is precisely the foreign partners' principal contribution. The convertible currency contribution is usually a component part used mainly as circulating capital at the stage of organization. In some cases no convertible currency or only a small amount is contributed. The Russian side usually pays for the buildings and installations and the right of land use, and contributes the currency.

A somewhat different situation arises when the foreign investor buys a share of stocks in an already operating enterprise thus becoming a co-owner. An enterprise that is transformed into a joint-stock or limited liability company usually prefers to get convertible currency, which enables it to buy good enough equipment or necessary resources. To attract foreign capital, Chapter 5, "The Purchase of Shares in Enterprises, Stocks, and Other Securities by Foreign Investors", states that a company is viewed as using foreign investment if the foreign investor has paid for shares or stocks with foreign currency.

When establishing the rate at which foreign currency is converted into roubles, it should not be the form, type of currency with which stares or stocks of the transformed or privatized company is bought but the methods of the latter's valuation, which are presently non-existent. Naturally enough, residual balance value of the fixed assets cannot be used for this purpose.

The law establishes that all foreign currency expenses involved in the establishment and functioning of an enterprise using foreign investments, including the transfer of the foreign investor's profits abroad, are to be paid for by its own foreign currency revenues for the type of activity it engages in, as well as by foreign currency obtained from other legal sources. To provide a favorable environment for the work of such companies, it has been established that all foreign currency yielded by the exports of an enterprise's own produce stays at its disposal. This is also true of the so-called "domestic exports", i.e., the sales of produce for foreign currency in the country's territory.

So as to stop the illegal demands that the joint ventures use foreign currency to pay for goods and services manufactured by other companies in the country's territory, Article 22 of the Law on Foreign Investments in the RSFSR permits the companies with foreign participation to use roubles to purchase goods and services in the market of the Russian Federation (including rent for living quarters and premises).

THE PROCEDURE FOR THE PURCHASE OF SECURITIES BY FOREIGN INVESTORS

For a foreign investor to purchase stock (and to set up a new joint venture), information about the foreign partner, copies of the articles of association or the charter of the joint venture, etc. is to be submitted to the pertinent body. Is such tight control really necessary, especially as securities are bound to change hands more and more often as market relations advance? In the future, the only condition may be to register the transaction at the local fiscal body, which would officially attest to the type of currency used in it (so as to establish the organizational and legal status of the company in question). If the foreign investor pays with roubles, the legality of their purchase should be checked.

A simpler procedure would make it easier to attract foreign capital. For the time being, there is hope that it will be streamlined as the laws on stock markets and stock market transactions involving foreign investors are drawn up and passed (at least as concerns market trade in securities).

TRADE FOR FOREIGN CURRENCY AND FOR ROUBLES

Under the law, joint ventures are permitted to trade only in their own produce. To sell goods purchased abroad for foreign currency, they need permission to engage in brokerage (obtainable from the republics' central banks). The fee is payable in convertible currency and constitutes 10% of the overall volume of foreign-currency sales. It is also depends on the share of cash in the payments, the share of the company's own produce in the overall volume of foreign-currency sales, and the rouble part of the volume of sales. Since the rouble is officially recognized as the only legal means of payment, the fee is charged for "undermining" it in the national market; it goes into the foreign currency intervention fund and is sold in the domestic currency market so as to boost the rouble exchange rate.

This step could also help monitor the movement of goods crossing the state frontier. As is known, the companies importing goods sold for foreign currency into the Commonwealth do not pay the import charge. If such goods are sold for roubles, the import charge is to be paid within 10 days of the sale in the domestic market. Failure to pay the charge into the budget entails a late charge (0.2% daily). But at the moment the customs de not have a definite and reliable system of supervision, as a result of which the state is losing billions.

Should retail trade establishments selling goods for foreign currency be obliged to turn in accounts including the above-mentioned figures, the situation could be drastically changed. Under such a system, the companies would be directly interested in stating all their rouble sales in order to minimize the charges for foreign-currency retail trade. At the same time, the freight customs declarations usually state maximum amounts of goods subject to sales for foreign currency. It would thus be enough to obtain from the companies information about the carry-overs of goods at the warehouses, and an efficient system of after-the-customs supervision would be there, if, of course, the two departments succeed in coordinating their work and the process is automated and computerized.

The charge for foreign-currency trade is also extended to warehouse sales. The reason is that alongside with retail trade proper, a habit is being made of "show-room" trade, that is, selection of samples and sales of small consignments of selected articles straight from the warehouse. This is usually how small companies earning convertible currency purchase consumer goods for their employees. It does not make sense for them to get directly in touch with foreign suppliers. Extending the above-mentioned procedure to such transactions appears logical enough, the latter being a version of retail trade.

The Currency Market

At the moment, the only legal way to sell and purchase foreign currency is through the Center of Interbank Currency Transactions (the currency market), which deals chiefly in the sale and purchase of foreign currency, providing quotation for the current rouble market rate towards foreign currencies, and promoting its maintenance.

The currency market may operate either on its own behalf and at its own expense, or on behalf of clients as a broker (brokerage for commission).

The rouble is not very likely to become freely convertible since 1992. The most debatable point is the demand that exporter companies sell their foreign currency revenues to commercial banks at the market rate on obligatory basis, and the abolition of all foreign currency accounts.

There are also proposals for partial or external convertibility of the rouble, which is counted upon to attract foreign investments and stimulate international economic cooperation generally by giving the foreigners more reliable guarantees that they would be able to convert the roubles they have earned into hard currency. There are plans for a special fund formed, in part, with the means of Western states, whose governments would, in fact, be guarantors of free transfer of their investors' profits out of Russia. This forms of economic aid to Russia and the other ex-Union republics is favored by other countries, too.

Joint ventures, which have already made a place for themselves in the national economy, have good future prospects. Located at the junction of domestic and foreign economic fields, they are especially sensitive to economic and legal instability. The principal condition of their success would be a single legal framework of economic activities, the establishment of a new economic union, a single currency, and coordinated policies in the fields of finances, taxation, the issue of credits to finance foreign economic operations, and currency regulation. Success in dealing with this problem will determine the feasibility of foreign investments.

THE IMMEDIATE PRIORITIES

Nikolai Shmelev, Ph.D (Econ.)
Institute of the
United States of America and Canada

The crisis which has seized the Russian economy has, in essence, taken everyone unawares, including our economic science. The latter has never taken into account the most important question - the behavioral motivations of the producer and the natural conditions of an unhindered motion of the basic factors of production. Our economic findings and recommendations resembled an attempt to erect an Eiffel Tower on a swamp without a foundation: we were oblivious (and still are) of the existence of an objective commensuration of the labor input; of the success criteria; of the genuine success incentives; and of the feedback between an economic decision and its outcome.

Today, when we are faced by the threat of an overwhelming national catastrophe, life returns us to common sense inherent to man regardless of the gods to which society in which he lives in prays. At present all attention should be focused on the elementary, which has been known as longs as civilization, progress, economic growth and expanded production exist: how to secure a normal blood circulation in the economic organism of the country and how to revive in our society the incentives for normal and conscientious labor.

But the unique and dramatic feature of our present situation in the fact that as the crisis deepens, the purely economic factors are pushed to the background. The country's economy is becoming to be determined, on an increasing scale, by non-economic forces: political ambitions, the zeal and vanity of the leaders, their honesty or, on the contrary, dishonesty and heartlessness, the irrational behavior of the demonstrating crowds, the influence of various chimeras such as old ethnic hostility and claims, fears and the deteriorating psychological state of the masses.

It is obvious that neither the present day social system, nor its chief element - the economic crisis - can be described and explained by purely economic categories. Just the same, the way out of this crisis depends, unfortunately, not only on economic measures.

Not economic farsightedness is imperative today, but actions analogous to those of a fireman rescuing a burning house. If we manage to bring to a halt the disastrous recession of the economy and somehow normalize the situation, afterwards we will have enough time to think out a strategy for the revival and the radical renewal of the country. And it does not matter how that new society in which we will live will be called.

The "firemen" who are trying to save our house are faced by three major problems: restoring the ruble's competence; privatization; creating a social "security network" capable of preventing the country from exploding. In addition, as during a fire, all this must be accomplished simultaneously, no matter how difficult it may seem. The ruble cannot be revived without privatization and without an effective social anesthesia needed for the performance of such painful surgery. Privatization alone will be futile if universal barter prevails in the country like during the stone age, and if the understandable envy of the impoverishing crowd to the successful entrepreneurs is not kept back by some compensation measures. But, in turn, the crowd will never be able to overcome its present semi-hungry state if the ruble does not start working to a full extent and entrepreneurship is granted complete freedom.

The problem of restoring the ruble's competence is the general problem of all republics and states constituting today's "ruble zone", including the Baltic republics. I am positive that the issue by any republic of its own non-convertible national currency (it cannot be convertible from the very start under any conditions) will, in fact, be a declaration of an economic war to Russia and the first step towards a general civil war. And this war will be caused by the reckless policy and complete economic ignorance of the new politicians and by the insanity of the crowd which will, in the end, be the one to pay dearly on all accounts. And that may happen very soon.

Common defense and common economy - without this minimum the very existence of the new commonwealth of states which has appeared on the ruins of the former Soviet Union is impossible. A common economy and common market space inevitably imply: a common banking system; common targeted funds; a common budget regardless of its size.

The complete revival of the ruble's competence during the initial state depends on the success in the three major spheres: a balance between demand and supply on the market, i.e., between the aggregate mass of currency and the commodity supply; the elimination or a sharp reduction of the budget deficit, bringing to a minimum money emission and the limitation of the banks' loan expansion; liquidation of the tremendous mass of "empty money" which has accumulated during the past few years as a result of the irresponsible and suicidal government policy of unrestrained inflationary financing.

In the conditions of a continuing sharp recession of production (it will not stop until money begins to work on a full scale) it is possible to restore the balance between the mass of currency and the supply of goods only if a complete liberalization of wholesale and retail prices is carried out. But in our concrete conditions, given our level of social tension, Russia and the other republics will have to learn to leave with hyperinflation for some time (not less than one year).

The price level in our economy, including the price for labor, will inevitably grow in the nearest future by 10 or maybe by 100 times. This will happen because once the process of liberalization begins, it is impossible to check it. And the liberalization of prices for all products, including prices for fuel and raw materials is only a question of time.

I understand the fears of some economists that the unprecedented monopolization of our economy in conditions of a free market will enable the monopolistic enterprises to artificially rise prices. I believe this is unavoidable, even if necessary taxation measures against monopolistic profits from price rises will be taken timely. But in any economy, and in ours as well, there exists a certain invisible ceiling after reaching which even monopolistic prices will have to start climbing down. Proof to this is our own economic experience - the famous "sales crisis" of 1923 - which occurred a year after the introduction of the new economic policy. In the present conditions the point is whether the system of social relations in the country will be able to hold out till the beginning of such a "sales crisis".

The liberalization of prices will do nothing for the restoration of the ruble and the stabilization of the market, if the problems of our monstrous budget deficit will not be solved simultaneously.

Three types of budget receipts play the greatest role in replenishing the common budget: the republics' payments; taxes; the sale of state property. The Union budget had been destroyed mainly by the republics and they are the ones who should restore it, if they want their political or economic union to survive. This equally concerns all the republics and their most vital interests. Uzbekistan, which, for example refuses to enter 11 billion rubles into the Union budget, deprives itself of budget subsidies of a minimum of 14 billion rubles without which it cannot exist. Of course, it would have been better to introduce, as it gas been done all over the world, a mutually agreed federal or confederate tax. Or at least establish a system of fixed payments.

The liberalization of prices will also increase the budget's receipts, firstly, as a result of the inevitable lagging behind of the free wage growth from the free price growth. The tax on added value and various excises shall also play a significant role, if only the state manages to reestablish, during the shortest possible period, what it has destroyed - the normal trade of goods subject to excise. The scale of taxes on the population's incomes should be changed drastically not as much from the budget point of view, as from the social point of view. In 1992 a 1000 ruble monthly income will probably be lower than any subsistence minimum. The size of the medium and high incomes will be changed, accordingly.

It is my opinion that the tax on profit cannot exceed 35% and that all investments should be tax free. However, not less than 90% of profit, exceeding the mean size of profitability (at least for the coming year) should be channelled to the budget: it is obvious that in the existing conditions in most cases superprofits cannot be acquired through new technologies, but are merely a result of a monopolistic inflation of prices. The time has come to introduce tax exemptions for all producers of agricultural goods. One must bear in mind that the 10% tax on producers had strongly boosted agricultural production in the early 1920s in Russia.

It is almost impossible to regain a budgetary balance in the existing extreme conditions without an intensified sale of state assets and surplus supplies amassed by the state enterprises and also without the issue of long-term state-loan bonds with a mobile interest dependable on the inflation rate. In this case the budget will receive hundreds of billion of rubles which will give a chance to overcome the existing deficit. There is also a possibility to quickly expand the tax foundation of the budget at the cost of privatization and the growth of private initiative and entrepreneurship. In any case, many countries had gone through budget crises and had always found a way to cope with it.

At the same time, no one ever succeeded in reviving a budget without a sharp decrease of budgetary spending. The basic directions of such a decrease are the following: cutting down military spending and, especially, the purchase of conventional armaments; terminating the subsidizing of disadvantageous enterprises both in industrial and agricultural production; decreasing the scope of capital construction and transferring most of it from budget financing to credit financing; lowering our foreign debts; curtailing administrative spending. And we must face the truth: any serious attempts to improve the social position of any considerable stratum of the population during the transition period is impossible for the country's economy. At best we should strive to preserve a level a fraction higher than elementary physical existence.

However, money in our country will not become money until another pressing problem in not solved: the elimination of the surplus mass of currency held by the population and the enterprises. Only part of it (and the smaller part) has an investment purpose and can be reduced through the sale of shares, bonds, unmarketable products, excess supplies, apartments, land, etc. Another part is the "hot money" intended for the purchase of consumer goods, thus creating their shortage. Of course, part of this "hot money" will shrink as a result of the liberalization of prices and hyperinflation. But it is hard to believe that in our country, with its extremely tense social situation, the government can liberalize retail prices for all goods without granting inflationary compensations to the population's bank accounts.

The country will not be able to cope with the accumulated surplus money without an intense commodity intervention which can be attained in the following way: encouraging the manufacture of consumer (in the first place costly) goods in the course of converting defense plants into consumer goods plants; temporarily curtailing investment import and shifting the freed hard currency means to the import of consumer goods; liberalization of import and a purposeful encouragement of all its forms, including the primitive, but very necessary at the present moment, barter; the unobstructed duty free (of course, temporarily) import of any consumer goods; and, finally, (and perhaps the most important) obtaining special loans on international financial markets directed towards solving this extraordinary problem - the elimination of "hot money". In essence, all this is already being carried out or is beginning to be carried out. The point is whether we will succeed before our economy collapses entirely under the pressure of the increasing output of the money-printing machine.

Our economy can be considered completely recuperated only when the ruble will become fully convertible. Russia's leadership intends to achieve at least a partial convertibility of the ruble by the middle of this year. I think that we should not be too optimistic in this respect. The sick ruble, in contrast to the potential possibility of issuing a parallel currency (i.e., the "chervonets", but this a separate issue) can become convertible only when the objective proportions in our internal prices will be at least approximately revived; when inflation will be checked and, what is most important, the population and enterprises will once again begin to trust the ruble. Otherwise no budget reserves will be enough to maintain the free convertibility of the ruble.

The next immediate priority is privatization. But I am afraid that in the existing situation we might again chose the wrong path: we are too concerned about what to do with our industrial giants and, in general, with the large-scale and medium state property. Indeed, it needs to be privatized, but in the course of several years and maybe even decades. It is my belief that today these enterprises need only one thing: full economic independence and with the right of attracting additional investment resources through gradually turning them into joint-stock companies and issuing stocks to the free market.

Our economy and market can emerge from their present coma condition through other means: first, leasing or selling at auctions all minor and if there are customers, all average state industrial, trade and servicing enterprises to become privately or collectively owned; second, opening new private or cooperative enterprises in all spheres of the economy on a strictly legal registration principle (in contrast to the permission principle); third, the liquidation of hopelessly unprofitable collective and state-run farms and handing over their land into full ownership of farmers with the right of its subsequent free sale and purchase.

Precisely such an approach had ensured the rapid revival of the almost breathless Soviet economy in the mid 1920s. These are those mushrooms which spontaneously, by their sheer natural creative force, break through the thick of the pavement by which our administrative system has tightly bounded our economic life. And it is unsurprising that today the new "democratic" bureaucracy, along with all state and underground criminal structures, is desperately resisting any tangible steps towards such privatization.

Hence it is clear what is to be done. But will our country, our rapidly disintegrating society survive such a painful surgical operation? I think that no one today can provide a definite answer to this question. Some things remain unclear: the extent of the political insanity that has gripped the country, the mood of the silent majority, and how much the people can tolerate. But at least in the economic sphere the general outline of a social "security network" has become visible: this is, first, the urgent efforts to fill the consumer market at any cost, including loans; second, liberalizing wages along with prices; third, an indexation of the fixed incomes of the population in at least an approximate accordance with the inflation rate; fourth, a more or less fair compensation of the devaluating bank accounts and a refusal to freeze or confiscate these accounts; fifth, an elaborated strategy and tactics against the most dreadful threat which is looming on the horizon - the inevitable unemployment growth.

Everything points to the fact that this year will decide everything. Either our new politicians, especially those on a republican level, will come to their senses and will join their efforts in introducing the long-awaited economic reforms, and these reforms will at least stabilize the economy which will give us a chance to start climbing out of the hole, or, if this does not happen, we will be thrust into a state of complete chaos as was the case in the early 17th century during the time of the Great Disturbance or in the year 1917.

In conditions of a normal market the role of the state boils down to removing all obstacles on the way of the capital, commodities, ideas and people. Until that neither the people, nor enterprises, nor society can be granted neither real sovereignty, nor democracy, even if they are declared formally. Our salvation will begin when the economy begins to change.

THE OIL CRISIS IN THE COMMONWEALTH OF INDEPENDENT STATES

Mikhail Surtsukov

It was forecast 15 years ago both by the native "prophets" and "CIA misinformants", but even now, when we are tumbling down into its widely opened jaws, nothing is being done to avert a catastrophe.

This introduction may appear too emotional. But let us take a look at sober facts and figures.

In 1991, oil production in the Commonwealth of Independent States was 518 million tons as compared to 624 million tons in the best years, 1987-1988.

The Economic Ministry's forecast for 1992 was about 480 million, the CIA's, 460 million, and V.Neverov's (the oil king of the Hermes company), 410 million tons. The spread is wide enough but, given the prevalent trend, immaterial: all these prognostications will come true, even if with intervals of a few months.

What do these figures mean? 450 million tons is roughly the domestic consumption in the Commonwealth.

Can it be cut down without serious damage to the economic situation in the member-states?

Although petroleum products are not always used thriftily enough, in many cases overconsumption stems from the low technological production level, which would take more than a few months to update. And physical shortage of oil products entails losses that are hundreds of times greater than any known cost of the latter's purchase. This is known well enough in the countries that have flourishing economies, and precisely for this reason stable physical deliveries are the top priority of their oil policies. This is why in the 1970s, certain quarters in the United States even covertly encouraged the rise of oil prices in the world market viewing it as a way to restore the current and long-term petroleum balance in their own country and in the world economy generally.

This means that the answer to the question formulated above is no.

Towards the end of our century or the beginning of the next Russia (in fact, the only net exporter of oil among the ex-republics) will have, at best, to stop selling oil for convertible currency, and, in the worst but not impossible case, to begin importing it, so as to satisfy the minimal needs of the Commonwealth members, if, of course, it still exists by that time.

But is this feasible, what with Russia's foreign debts and the fact that it urgently needs to import a number of essential goods? Probably not.

If Russia is forced to further contract its oil deliveries to the Commonwealth states (a matter which is already breeding conflicts), they will soon feel the catastrophic consequences of petroleum shortages and will have to buy oil in the world market. Ukraine's negotiations with Kuwait are only the beginning.

This new situation will, first, sharply weaken the attractions of the Commonwealth for oil importers, and, second, make certain political circles ask why the ex-republics can find convertible currency to pay other exporters but not Russia. Relations inside the Commonwealth will become even tenser.

In 1991, oil output in Russia was about 460 million tons as compared to 515 million tons in 1990, and will be about 400 million tons in 1992. The epicenter of the crisis is the Tyumen Region, where the production level dropped from a high of 394 million tons in 1988 to 318 million tons in 1991, and, according to some estimates, will be only about 260 million tons in 1992. The situation is the worst in the area of Samotlor: oil production at the Nizhnevartovsk Oil and Gas Company, the biggest one in the country only a short while ago, went down from 163 million tons in 1985 to 61 million tons in 1991, and, says its head manager V.Palii, will be only 27 million tons in 1992.

Outside Western Siberia, things are not yet quite as desperate. There, output is either stable or is declining at a relatively lower pace and is even growing a little at some companies. A similar situation prevails outside Russia: in Kazakhstan, oil production is rising.

But stability is only temporary: if radical steps are not taken the other oil-producing regions will be hit just as badly.

If things stay the same, by early 1995 oil output in Russia will decline to about 300 million tons, barely enough for domestic consumption. And it is highly unlikely that it will continue to sell any oil to the Commonwealth members for roubles while paying dollars to purchase oil for itself in the world market, if only because it will simply have no dollars.

It is also unlikely that Ukraine will export enough competitive goods and services to earn about $6 billion to buy the 40 million tons of oil it needs in the world market. The same goes for Belarus, which would need $2.3 million tons to pay for 15 million tons of oil.

Thus, if the present trends in the Russian oil producing industry persist, both it and the other Commonwealth members are in for a difficult time.

Why have things gone from bad to worse in this field?

Not because the oil deposits are exhausted, and not because some other mining or geological factors have interfered. Experts assert that a more than 10-13% oil production decline is practically technologically impossible even at individual deposits even if their past exploitation was incompetent. Neither can one say that proved reserves are small. Since the mid-1940s, the extent of provision with proved deposits in the USA 10-12 years, and yet output was either maintained at the same level or even rose. Only after the US territory was surveyed ten times more thoroughly than Russia, the indicator of proved reserves went down to eight-nine years, and output began to slowly decline. According to different estimates, the figure for Russia is 12-18 years, and the probability of discovering new deposits is much higher than in the United States: nearly a half of Russia's vast territory is potentially oil-bearing and very inadequately surveyed.

A "contribution" to the Russian oil crisis was, of course, made by the under-deliveries of equipment after the collapse of the USSR, but even these two factors operating together cannot explain the present pace of the decline.

What remains, then, are economic factors, and if the situation in oil production is regarded from this angle, many things become much clearer.

Considering the prices for other goods and services, the 350 roubles which the oil workers receive per ton of oil often do not cover even exploitation costs. People are leaving for more lucrative jobs. The oil prices do not bring in enough money to prospect and launch new deposits, which alone can stop the production slump. Companies in Komi have already gone on strike; a 350-rouble rise, which is supposed to satisfy the industry's employees, is being negotiated. But the expected inflation rates will make even this figure too low in only a few months.

Both local and sectoral leadership in the oil and gas producing regions realize that the industry's financial straits are artificially fabricated, and that the way out of the crisis depends almost entirely on the economic policy of the Russian leadership. But the latter's steps have not convinced the oil and gas industry bosses that if in the next one to three years output remains at an acceptable level, the oil prices will be raised as high as the oil workers would like them to be.

In the present situation the industry will most probably do enough to counter the production decline to avoid being accused of inaction but certainly not as much as it could do, using the slump to put pressure to bear on the central (now Russian) authorities.

In the mid-1980s, some American companies bought up the stock of other companies owning land rich in oil but did not hurry to begin exploitation in the expectation that in five-seven years the dollar prices for oil would go up 1.5-2 times. In the case of Russia, the current rouble and dollar prices differ 60 times!!! From the economic viewpoint, the tactic of not trying too hard is more than justified: when profitability is low and even negative, there is no sense producing too much of the stuff, which in the nearest future can be confidently expected to become infinitely more expensive.

Apart from the decline of output and the damage to the economy in general (which stems from the shortage of petroleum products and is difficult to assess), the policy of constantly keeping the state prices for oil at a level that is killing the industry is fraught with other adverse consequences.

The industry's hard financial position robs it of direct access to up-to-date technologies and equipment, obliging it to attract investors who could supply them, mainly foreign ones. But in the present situation this is an expensive enough business, because under the contracts that have already been signed about a half of the oil produced by joint ventures goes to pay for the services and profits of Western partners.

This has happened because:

- first, the Western partners have to be compensated for the high risks they are taking in a politically unstable situation;
- second, Russia has a very imperfect investment law and no oil law that would take into account the rental nature of the branch (such law exists in practically all countries exporting oil and petroleum products);
- third, the bodies conducting negotiations and signing contracts with Western partners are not competent enough;
- fourth, there is a high level of corruption in society.

Simple analysis shows that if the favorable terms currently given to foreign companies are expanded, and oil production goes back to the 500-million-ton mark by producing a half of this amount at joint ventures, 120-130 million tons will go away as payment for the services of foreign partners. Obviously, the remainder will be not only insufficient to give Russia enough hard currency in return for oil exports and to satisfy the needs of the ex-Union republics, but to meet either of these targets taken separately.

To maintain the present approach to price formation in the fuel and energy industry would be akin to starving a hen laying gold eggs is starved so that it would stop producing, and giving the grain it consumes to an idler. Between 1988 and 1992, oil production in Russia dropped by about 150 million tons. Thus, the annual losses sustained by 1992 can be estimated at $18 billion, or more than three trillion roubles by the current exchange rate, a sum that is more than enough to cover the country's budget deficit.

The relatively low prices for fuel and energy, above all, for the easy-to-export oil and petroleum products, are extremely conducive to corruption in society at large and especially in the top echelon. Despite the fact that the procedure for the issue of export licenses for oil and petroleum products has been made more complex and the export charges are high enough, oil transactions remain a very profitable foreign trade operation. The high efficiency of the exports as compared to the domestic economy leads to bribery, when millions of dollars or several hundred million roubles change hands. These sums are large enough to break the psychological resistance of almost anyone, and it is not surprising that, according to the press, in the very first month of the new year the amount of oil for which export licenses were issued exceeded Russia's physical export potential.

It is extremely dangerous to preserve the gap between the domestic and the export price because this corrupts the decision-makers' mentality; instead of promoting a rational market economy abiding by the rules of honest competition such mentality may help build an inefficient half-state/half-mafia system.

In the present situation the only way out of the quickly mounting oil and energy crisis in Russia and the Commonwealth generally is to sharply raise the prices for fuel and energy, maybe even to the world level. A year ago, I was still against such a course believing it could be postponed, but since then the situation has deteriorated so far that urgent steps must be taken. This is also what Western experts recommend and what Gaidar seems to realize, judging by his interviews. It is, however, obvious that such a step is bound to have serious political repercussions and can be decided upon only at the highest political level. It does not have an alternative but, if the energy and fuel supply deteriorates at the expected pace the economic situation in the Commonwealth will certainly not improve.

Unless the current trend is reversed, by the beginning of 1995 oil production in the country may drop to 360-380 million tons, that is, to four-fifths of the present consumption level. The adverse effect of the physical shortage of oil increases exponentially; American experts say that with a shortage of 20% the country's GNP would drop commensurately, and at 40%, economic collapse may ensure. In our situation, what with suppressed consumption of oil and petroleum products and the share of industrial consumption exceeding than in the USA, the adverse effect of oil shortages on the economy will mount faster and be even more painful.

The chief arguments in favor of state-regulated and relatively low oil and energy prices is the fear of an inflationary effect and the population's and enterprises' inability to withstand a sharp rise of these prices. But this approach ignores some major circumstances:

- world fuel and energy prices operate in practically all countries with the exception of the poorest African states lying south of Sahara, where the budget subsidizes only the prices for kerosene used for lighting and cooking (and even that chiefly to prevent the nomads from burning out the remaining vegetation in the savannah thus causing the desert to spread farther into the continent);
- in most industrialized countries (except the USA) world prices are complemented by excise duty for gas and petroleum products reaching two-thirds of the world

price, and if retail prices incorporating such excise are too high for us, we should confine ourselves to world wholesale prices;

- raising the fuel and energy prices to world level (while still licensing their export) simultaneously sharply boosts production and reduces consumption. We have enormous untapped potential in both spheres: according to some estimates, this step could raise oil output by 30-40 million in the next six months in annual terms in relation to the current level, and cut down the consumption of these products by about the same amount. This would make it possible to increase the export of oil thus greatly easing the problem of our foreign debt, importing essential goods, and returning the rouble rate to a relatively realistic level;
- given adequate legislation that would regulate the rental payments efficiently enough, establishment of the fuel and energy prices at roughly the world level would give the government a major and, what is more, a disguised source of budget revenues enabling it to fix a somewhat lower taxation rate than it would have to introduce otherwise;
- a large and healthy sector able to eventually cure the others would be formed in the Russia economy;
- in price formation, a more or less stable area (world prices do fluctuate in the annual range of 10-25%) making the other prices more balanced would be created;
- it would become easier to go over to world correlation of prices in the domestic economy generally, thus helping the Russian economy to get integrated into the world economy;
- the ex-republics would, in the end, find it easier to supply their goods to the Russian market at rouble world prices in exchange for Russian oil than to buy oil in the world market with dollars earned by exporting their goods.

Without question, the fuel and energy prices cannot be freed without a revision of the existing legal and organizational infrastructure. The first thing to be done is to create an efficient mechanism to compensate the rise of the fuel and energy prices to the population and certain industries.

PRIVATIZATION VS PRIVATE PROPERTY

Oleg Pchelintsev, Cand.Sc.(Econ.)
Institute of National Economic Forecasting
Russian Academy of Sciences

One must note the following paradox: the International Monetary Fund and three other organizations which have prepared a report on the transition to a market economy in our country (USSR Economy. A study of the USSR economy on the request of the Houston conference participants, Moscow, International Foundation "Cultural Initiative", 1991) suggest, as the first and most important step, not an "overwhelming Privatization", but a commercialization of the state sector enterprises - which means full economic independence obedient to strict financial limitations.

This does not mean that the authors of the report are against Privatization. The report focuses on one notion, among others, that before a market is established it is impossible to correctly evaluate the enterprises' assets, i.e., otherwise Privatization becomes a lottery. But most important is another conception (not named, but implied): a serious and responsible attitude towards property. In their understanding Privatization has nothing to do with the credo: "Take everything and divide it!"

It is technically impossible to divide equally among all citizens the country's capital and land: those not born will be left out. And economically this is a heavy blow to savings: the dividends, dispersed among millions of families, will merely become an addition to one's salary. Besides, the very spirit of this procedure is anti-market, since the absolute law of the market is compensation. And we want to begin with a gigantic presentation of property.

Is It Possible to Sell State Property?

At first glance is seems that the sale of state property is faultless. However, in reality it will lead not to entrepreneurship (that is what we want to achieve), but to dividend collecting, in essence. In addition, the potential demand for property is estimated at 100-150 million rubles, while the total cost of the basic state assets is 2 trillion rubles. Thus, any redemption is out of the question, at least during the coming several years. First, in the conditions of inflation the cost of the basic assets should be re-estimated. Second, during a transition to a market economy the bulk of the population and most of the enterprises will only possess enough means for the purchase of items of prime necessity. Third, even if these free means appear, taking into account the conditions of competition, they will have to be channelled to scientific and technological research.

Privatization and the Market

Many people regard Privatization not as a means of transferring to a market economy, but as a means of protecting themselves against it. Not by chance does Privatization acquire most ugly forms. State property is liquidated in a crude and irresponsible way, the same as private property was liquidated after the revolution (as was noted by J.Kornai, a prominent Hungarian economist).

In reality there is no close link between Privatization and the market. In order to transfer to a market economy it is enough to lease a part of the state enterprise, to form a "national leasing system" (according to the terminology of the head of the well-know consulting firm PlanEcon).

This is especially important from the legal point of view, since in our country there had practically never existed other property than state property. Any attack on state property in present-day conditions serves to destroy the remaining sense of justice.

A successful transition to a market economy will be possible to the same degree to which we will be able to preserve and develop our attitude towards state (as well as to all other forms) property as to something sacred and inviolable. In other words, the acknowledgment of the equality of private property with other forms of property has nothing to do with the idea of the total offensive against state property.

Many economists and politicians in our country view Privatization as some universal method equally applicable to production, the infrastructure and the social sphere of both the commercial and non-commercial sections. This was revealed in the adoption of "via" laws on Privatization and chiefly in the calculations of the cost of the privatized property, when the capitals of different branches are simply combined, disregarding their market profitability and the presence (or absence) of natural monopolies. And this is not surprising: the economists, as well as the law-makers do not understand and are unaware of such crucial phenomena as external benefit, social goods, declining maximum expenses about which their colleagues in the west have been concerned for decades. Precisely these "black holes" of the market mechanism determine the necessity of a differentiated approach towards the above-mentioned spheres, refusing some of them not only Privatization, but even commercialization.

The lack of legally regulated non-commercial (non-profit) organization may have especially damaging consequences, since this is the key sphere for the development of the social sphere and charity in the West.

It is indicative that Privatization is only linked with the property for the means of production, while such a complex problem as the property of the ready product is being neglected. Thus, amidst the discussions on Privatization the bulk of the commodity assets is being seized by administrative bodies - from republics to local soviets.

A modern, scientifically-grounded solution of the question of property does not mean a simple choice of one of its forms (this is an out-dated approach), but a division of property's competence. It plays the same role in the economy as the division of powers in politics. Leasing must become a practical expression of this idea. Leasing is responsible for the successes of small businesses and the re-equipment of enterprises. In conditions of lease payments for state resources (capital interest and land rent) is the main source of replenishing the budget, but this means that a national leasing system could provide us with an economy with the lowest possible taxes.

It was a serious mistake of the first years of perestroika to reject payment for resources and to attempt to replace it by taxes, since it will be impossible to privatize the entire state property at one stroke: enterprises will have to operate on state land and capital for quite a while. To grant this land and capital actually free of charge as it is done now is an anti-market measure which has thrust the economy into a state of shock.

From the economic point of view, crushing the incentives of investing is the most critical problem created by "overwhelming' Privatization. Indeed, why should the entrepreneur spend means for new construction when he can obtain the necessary capital practically free-of-charge from the already existing state property? Therefore, capitalism as an obstacle to the accumulation of capital is another paradox bestowed upon us by "Privatization a la Soviet". Concerning the scope of state property in Russia and the aggressive nearsightedness of the "new entrepreneurs", the investment crisis may drag out for quite a while and be followed by the most gravest consequences.

This means that if we want to restore capital accumulation we must check the appropriation of state property. All those who wish to enrich themselves must: economize, protect and invest and cut down the number of lumpen "presentations"!

Therefore, not leasing, as many economists hold, but Privatization (not only the real, but the potential as well) is what is preventing our economy from acquiring capitalist features. Leasing solves this problem, creating a fund of credit resources for investment from lease payments. The next thing to be done is to overcome the "fear of lending" typical of work collectives, and here the state enterprises' administration must put its foot down.

The national leasing system--is not only a refusal of utopian quick and just Privatization, but a new state policy in economy which essence is: a transition from a state management of the economy to a state management of property.

Our newly-established committees (funds) of state property have been planned not as bodies for managing property, but, rather as liquidation commissions. The moment the state had finally found its niche in the economy, it was bound hand and foot.

PRIVATIZATION PROGRAM

The recently issued "Basic regulations of the program for the Privatization of state and municipal enterprises in the Russian Federation in 1992" confirm the above fears. It is a direct attempt to legalize the liquidation of state property. The document does not specify what the Committee on managing state property intends to do with that part of state property which will not be privatized although it amounts to 95% of the cost (not even the market cost, but the so-called remaining cost) of the basic assets. It is also not clear what profit and in what way will be derived from it and how it will be managed.

It is often said that the state is seized by a financial crisis and must urgently sell part of its property in order to survive. But why not receive lawful profits from its tremendous property instead of first giving it away as a gift and then becoming a pauper and increasing taxes on profits?

Hence the enterprises which have received a large amount of resources from the state (or those which spent all the profits for wages) turn out to be free of any financial obligations--because they have no profits and no sources for paying. And, on the contrary, those enterprises which did not receive anything from the state, say cooperatives, which work on their own capital, will have to pay the highest taxes, i.e., the old egalitarianism is being passed off as a restructuring of the economy.

This a result of the inability to understand Western experience, when taxes "work" in conditions of full payment for all resources and thus regulate the state's economic relations, firstly, with the non-state sector of the economy.

The state property must be managed not by branch structures, but by independent commercial organizations, arranged along territorial principles--regional holding-banks and investment funds.

And only after a network of such banks and funds is established and after the first experience of managing state property in market conditions is accumulated, can the question on the sale of ineffective property be considered. And that is when a Privatization program will be needed.

The above document contains another "bomb" - the entire range of relations between the privatized and non-privatized branches. "Jealousy" may become so strong that it may exceed reasonable limits and work will have be stopped until all relations are cleared up.

There is also a third obstacle - regional monopoly. In the process of devising territorial programs this issue must be in the forefront, and not the fulfillment of a priori, coming from the top, "average" Privatization showings.

How can one associate the bacchanal of the free giving away of state property with the mass bankruptcy of enterprises, what will the essence of the structural reshaping of the economy be during the stage of its transfer to a market economy? Some people will be getting 25% of shares and others, doing the same work, will be thrown out into the street?

The chief element of the Program is the "compulsory Privatization assignments" which in essence do not differ from the notorious collectivization assignments and attest to the authors' "planned approach to the market".

Thus, the "Privatization prior to a market" which is taking place at the present moment can only be a commanding-distributing operation. Actually, it even enhances the directive role of the state in the economy, because the bureaucracy is the one in charge of Privatization. This will become furthermore evident when the time will come to pay the promised dividends: the state will have to either start printing more money or admit that Privatization was a futile idea and has only created additional difficulties for the accumulation of capital. The same as collectivization at its time destroyed the institute of social property, the administrative Privatization campaign will sharply deteriorate the psychological climate in society and will nip in the bud the very idea of private property. Not by chance the former nomenclature supports it so enthusiastically, because it will win in any case: if Privatization works out it will be on the top thanks to its favorable initial position; if Privatization does not work out it will immediately shift to the "left" saying: "We warned you that all this talk about democracy and a market was nonsense!"

Making Use of Western Experience

What we really need (even more than humanitarian assistance and foreign investments) is the social and cultural experience of the West of which we are hardly aware of. Many people in Russia believe that the basic traits of the people who have created the modern Western civilization are greed, egoism and unscrupulousness. Our refined intellectuals, who are dreaming about capitalist patrons of art, admit that it will take two or three generations before the latter appear. It is hard to tell what other speculations have damaged our public mentality worse than these.

The point is that the real reason of Western success is quite opposite: it is the mass moral and psychological mastering of the spheres of work and entrepreneurship, filling the every-day activity with a moral and religious essence and the overcoming of egoism as a primitive feature of a person's nature.

The intellectuals' conviction that an economic and technological upsurge is possible without developing social morals is an extremely dangerous one. It links, in fact, with the immorality of the lumpen stratum and its contempt for the law of the powers that be.

Despite the fact that we have a young and, on the whole, competent government, there exists a danger that the actions from "the top" may fail because of a lack of independent and responsible market subjects. In other words, the supply mechanism will not work because of the weak business potential. The entire science of macro-economic regulating losses sense if the economy lacks a normal microlevel.

In these conditions the legally correct transition of state enterprises to commercial functioning could of great psychological significance. From the economic point of view this will be agreements leasing state capital and land to work collectives.

THE REFORMS ARE DOOMED

The most hazards await the reform where they are not expected. For example, much hope is placed on the liberalization of prices, but the authorities in the republics and regions (plus an absence of a market infrastructure, plus a gigantic sector of closed and semi-closed trade) will not let it take place. Free prices will only attract a handful of outsiders who will be immediately neutralized by the trade mafia and racketeers. Free trade must be backed by a legislation and that is what we do not have.

Another negative factor is the above-mentioned lack of a mechanism of capital accumulation. As it is known, our economy developed along compulsory lines and as soon as the managing departments collapsed it turned out that there was nothing that could replace them: the country entered an investment crisis, whose consequences are more grave than the disintegration of the consumer market.

However, not even this is the most frightful thing. What is worse is a lack of motivation inherent to a normal market. Our producer is oriented not towards making a maximum profit, but towards a "peaceful" life with an adequate profit. And that is why he will respond to any price rise not by expanding production, but by curtailing production.

This danger is especially visible in agricultural production. By distributing the land we will be left not with farmers (as many economists hope), but with a traditional peasant, one even more traditional than those prior to the beginning of collectivization, because he lacks many necessary skills.

Let us imagine that the dreams of privatization champions have come true: each citizens has received a checkbook which he has exchanged for stocks. What will happen next? For the majority of the people nothing will happen at all, while the most active ones will gather an at annual meeting of the share-holders which will, in fact, turn into a rally. After making some noise, the participants will go home, having got nothing for their pains. This will be a situation of private ownership without personal responsibility; the managers will be free to do anything they like.

As for taxes on property many of our citizens regard them as something hostile and useless.

It will not be easy to change such a mentality. We are still to create a normal stratum of the rich, who will not seek privileges from the state and will realize the essence of their position in society as of "driving belts" of universal payability, a live engine of investing and charity.

The primary question today is how to prevent profits from being "spent on food" and to ensure their normal accumulation. Against the background of the country's universal ill-management and parasitical attitude full property rights in Russian conditions lead to apathy and stagnation. It is absolutely necessary for 100% of interest and rents to be re-invested into production.

Unfortunately, our market is being formed "from nil" and that is why in many ways it resembles a market of rather the 19th century than the 20th. A type of market towards which we are moving seems to be too primitive for our economy -- a highly urbanized, with complex transportation networks, nuclear power engineering, outer space exploration and other "acceleration" traits. Naturally, this evolving "Soviet" market has nothing to do with the most complicated institutional structures of the Western economies.

The only way out of this dead end is an accelerated development of the "top floor" of market structures responsible for the movement of capital (more important than commodities) and a parallel formation of institutions amending and balancing our market in dealing with such issues as social development, ecology, culture, etc.

It is imperative, in particular, to preserve, under market conditions, the accessibility (for domestic producers) of scientific and technological information. In general, a cheap infrastructure, the land and scientific and technical information -- are the "three whales" on which (along with a free market of leasing capital and private initiative of work collectives) our future economy could boost.

A PAYMENTS UNION OR A STABILIZED ROUBLE?

Mikhail Glebov

SCOPE OF COMMODITY EXCHANGE

Specialization and grand scale -these were the two fundamental principles by which the Soviet leadership faithfully abided throughout the country's existence. The results of this policy are known well enough. Production of some types of goods was concentrated in just one or two regions and even enterprises, and the republics were obliged to swap, or they would have simply been unable to survive.

Since 1992 the inter-republican exchange of goods has been called "import" and "export". For Russia, its overall volume accounts for some 30% of GDP, for Ukraine the figure is twice as high, 60%, and for Armenia--as high as 110%. To provide a reference point, Great Britain's trade with the other EC members constitutes 22%.

Disruption of trade contacts would therefore mean collapse. The economic situation would deteriorate the most in the Commonwealth member-states that do not have much convertible currency.

TRADE AND FOREIGN CURRENCY

Suppose that there is enough convertible currency. But then it will be used to import Western goods. As a result, protectionist barriers will appear inside the Commonwealth, the volume of inter-republican trade will go down, and the economic crisis will deepen.

At the time of transition to the free market, trade among the Commonwealth members has to be brisk enough, but this will be possible if all of them use the same currency as the means of payment. When the Commonwealth was formed, the understanding was that this would be the rouble, but the agreement does not look very firm. Ukraine is already printing coupons and is planning to introduce a national currency.

Suppose that national currencies have been introduced. What next? A temptation to charge dollars, francs, and marks for exported goods. Inter-republican trade would thus receive a lethal blow even if each government declares its currency convertible and opens its frontiers for trade with all the world.

Is there a way out of the situation that is shaping? *Yes, there is, to set up a payments union similar to the Western European one formed after the Second World War.* This is feasible, provided that the republican currencies are convertible in current settlements.

The system is supposed to function in the following way. Enterprises will receive hard currency for the goods sold outside the Commonwealth and the importer's currency in inter-republican trade. Thus the exporters would be forced to exchange the hard currency at their disposal for local currency. The importers will have to use hard currency to pay for the goods purchased outside the Commonwealth (to do this, they must have a chance to exchange local currency for dollars), but will use local currencies to pay for the goods imported from the other Commonwealth states. After the settlements within the framework of the payments union, the republics with a favorable trade balance will be able to extend loans to the republics with a trade deficit. In conjunction with a system of multilateral non-currency settlements, this would significantly weaken the dependence on hard currency. The rules of the payments union must oblige the debtors to pay a part of the debt in hard currency. This system is not, of course, suitable for dealing with long-term tasks, having all the faults of an artificial structure built on the basis of partial convertibility. But during the transition period it may prove useful.

Experts feel that the greatest difficulty facing such a union would be to lure into it the republic with a large favorable trade balance, because the rules would oblige them to extend credits to the weaker partners. Of great importance is the stand of Russia, which will have a big advantage thanks to its oil deposits. If Russia manages to stabilize the rouble and convince the others that an alternative currency is not needed, a payments union may not be necessary.

INFLATION: THE SITUATION HAS GOTTEN OUT OF CONTROL

V.Gerashchenko
Central Bank of the Russian Federation

The government of Russia has decided to tighten the monetary and credit policy. But there has recently been no overproduction of any commodities. Why then use monetary methods to make their manufacture more expensive and complicated? In Russia, inflation is rising so fast not only due to objective reasons but also in consequence of government decisions. In the nearest future the budget will not be able to do anything in the matter of investments and taxation privileges. The issue of relations between the commercial banks and the Central Bank of Russia arises. Should the ex-republics' central banks pursue a restrictive policy towards the credit relations existing between the commercial banks and the state sector of the economy? Or should the Central Bank adopt a well-considered policy under which it would be able to maintain the manufacture of goods in demand in the market? There is also need to settle the issue of the emergence of new competitive producers and the division and sell-out of existing enterprises and companies. And if the commercial banks do not have enough resources, when and on what terms can they be financed, and what interest should be paid on deposit business?

It is the population that will form the basis for shaping a corresponding cost of credit. Proceeding from the rates of inflation mentioned in the press, the interest rate should be close to it. This would raise the cost of credit to values that would make the existence of any normal economic body impossible without doubling its price. The controversy between the attempts to establish the right cost of money and the interest rate and to define a credit policy, on the one hand, and the companies' fear of bankruptcy and of supply lagging eternally behind demand, on the other, is the Gordian knot that has to be cut in the nearest future.

P.Zhikharev (Savings Bank of the Russian Federation): The interest rate on the loans should be high enough because it gives incentives to the producer. But at the same time it spurs on inflation. The Savings Bank of the Russian Federation is forced to keep the interest rates high because its staff alone is nearly 200,000, with 40,000 establishments and eight million clients a day. I do not think the interest rate should be fixed "from above", by command. At the moment, what is making the banks anxious is that enterprises may become insolvent. It is getting risky for banks to give long-term loans. The effect of insolvency will be worse than that of price liberalization.

The issue of risk has not been considered enough, because there is no adequate banking law. Many farmers are asking for one-three million rouble loans. But they have nothing but willingness to work hard. And if before a credit of 100,000 roubles was huge, today it is not enough to buy cattle, buildings, and equipment.

V.Arefiev (Tsentrosoyuz): The cost of credits will hold back production and contribute to its further decline. The moment the government displays a wish to cool the overheated economy down, interest rates begin to go sharply up. In its time, the West went through the same stage. Prospective clients go away empty-handed, being unable to pay a 40-50% interest rate. We should think about introducing a preferential re-financing system, which has long proved efficient in the West. Under it, commercial banks grant loans to certain industries and enterprises thus earning the right to preferential financing by the Central Bank.

Ya.Dubenetskii (Promstroibank): One of the causes of the crisis was the banks' having to turn away from large investments. There can be no restructuring of the economy until we begin to invest in it. It is urgently necessary to give taxation privileges to investments and to work out a clear mechanism of this process.

E.Kalashnikova (Avtobank): At the moment, we cannot give loans on normal terms because the interest rates change virtually every month. There are no guarantees even for the loans issued for two or three months. Any rumors work against us. Over a week or two, banks are left virtually with nothing. Massive withdrawals from commercial banks are also provoked by organizations which promise their clients an annual interest of 40, 60 and even 100% per annum.

V.Arefiev (Tsentrosoyuzbank): The Central Bank must be independent from the government both de jure and de facto. But at the moment this is not so: although under the law the Central Bank *is* independent, the President of Russia heads the government, and thus the Central Bank falls within his sphere of influence.

V.Solovov (Central Bank): Our present problems are related mainly to the interest policy. The government is pursuing a line at stabilizing the rouble. The Central Bank is supposed to contain the growth of the money issue, because unregulated price-formation has begun. As of early April, non-payment throughout Russia was 800 billion roubles. The situation has got out of control. When no one wants to sell their produce at the existing prices, hyperinflation becomes unavoidable.

R.Salekhov (Mosbiznessbank): Under hyperinflation, the Central Bank would retain two chief functions: to control the money issue, and to supervise the performance of the commercial banks. The banks need large injections. We have built a chain of non-payment thus causing production to slump because we do not inject money into it. Emission is unavoidable, but there should be at least a measure of control over it. There is no sensible balance between medium-sized and large banks, which sprang into existence quite spontaneously. Neither is there an inter-bank consultation bureau, which cannot be established unless commercial banks sort our their relations.

A. Khandruev ("Reform" Foundation): One thing is clear: if commercial banks do not make their condition known, they will find themselves without clients. Provided that the government continues the line at a deficit-free budget, commercial banks should become the tractor that could pull our economy out of the crisis.

THE LAWS OF PRIVATIZATION

Tatiana Popova, Cand.Sc.(Econ.)
International Foundation for Promoting
Privatization and Foreign Investments

Privatization is going ahead. The time has come to scrutinize the results of its initial stage so as to define an efficient strategy of this reform of ownership.

Macroeconomically, privatization is pursuing three *goals*. It is a necessary condition for transition to the free market, helping as it does to shape the agents of market relations: free, independent producers competing with one another. This is the first goal. The second is to help each individual company and enterprise and the country's economy generally to function more efficiently. The third is to transfer the bulk of the functions of management and administration to the proprietor, which would relieve the state from the need to deal with matters that are not really its business and drastically improve the quality of management.

To attain these objectives, privatization should rest on a clearly defined legal and methodological basis. Life shows that laws and norm-setting documents are necessary but not sufficient to prevent privatization from unfolding spontaneously and in a hectic manner. The hopes generated by the declaration of various privatization programs will hardly be justified, since most of them merely declare the need for privatization and may provide reference points and make predictions but do not oblige anyone to take practical steps. In view of this, the efficiency of the changes depends largely on the competence of the persons entrusted with privatizing one company or another.

The relevant laws define the legal principles of privatization, including the approach to the changes, the possibility of legal persons' and individuals' participation in privatization, the degree to which the opinion of the so-called "work collective" (staff) should be obeyed, and the forms and methods of privatization.

THE PRINCIPLES OF THE CHANGES (PRIVATIZATION)

A heated debate of this issue in 1990-1991 revealed three approaches to privatization: selling state property to private owners; distributing it among the citizens free of charge; placing enterprise and company assets into the ownership of their work collectives.

Despite the numerous warnings against inevitable repercussions, in most republics (Russia, Lithuania, Kazakhstan, Moldova) the law regulates the privatization of a part of state property by issuing the citizens with special means of payment or opening investment accounts for them (the second approach). This signifies the victory of populism over economic sense. But the laws have already been passed, and more debates could be fully as harmful as populism.

Theoretically, the law on privatization implies the following scheme of future action:

- taking an inventory and valuing the means of production;
- determining the share of state property subject to privatization at each consecutive stage (year);
- determining the share in the latter of the property subject to privatization free of charge;
- determining the amount of payment means (size of special accounts) issued to each citizen;
- launching both types of privatization (selling and giving away).

But in all republics except Lithuania, privatization is proceeding in an entirely different way. In Russia, for instance, companies are being either sold or turned into joint-stock associations, and investment accounts are only occasionally mentioned in the press. As a result, the volume of state property is dwindling slowly but perceptibly, and it looks more and more likely that by the time when the giving away is due to begin there will be nothing to give away.

If the idea of privatization free of charge has been abandoned due to the inefficiency and the dangers of this approach, the law should be revised. From the standpoint of the goals of privatization, giving away some of state property would help attain the fist one, shaping market agents. As for the efficiency of the performance of companies and the economy as a whole, as well as raising the quality of economic management, they would be undermined by such consequences of "free" privatization as dispersal of property, the prevalence of "rentier" interests among small stockholders, obstacles in the way of foreign investments, etc.

THE MAIN ASPECTS OF PRIVATIZATION

For the main part, republican legal acts prohibit the purchase of property subject to privatization by legal persons whose registered capital contains a share of state property. The strictest is the Law on the Privatization of State and Municipal Enterprises in the RSFSR, which denies the right of purchase to legal persons whose registered capital comprises more than 25% of stock (shares) belonging to the state, local Soviets of People's Deputies, public organizations (associations), charities, and other public funds.

This point-blank refusal of the right to participate appears too categorical and, generally, questionable.

As for privatization practices, the laws often get violated: at the auctions held in Moscow, no one checked the registered capitals of prospective buyers.

All laws without exception provide for the possibility of forced privatization. This clause, which is not generally popular, testifies to the maturity of the law-makers and their readiness for reform. Indeed, forced privatization is more just, ensuring the priority of public interests over group ones. Furthermore, the realization of this clause does not go against the goals of privatization.

But in a country where the word "forced" arouses a host of unpleasant associations (suffice it to recollect collectivization of agriculture), forced privatization may well provoke a sharply hostile response. Both the Work Collectives' Union and the Independent Trade Unions of Russia oppose this policy.

Dealing with this issue, the republics' legislatures went widely diverging ways. Kazakhstan's law gives work collectives a priority right to buy, which means, essentially, that if the work collective agrees to take part in privatization, the other claimants to the right of ownership are automatically excluded.

Russia's approach is quite different. The form (or method) of privatization is established by the commission on the privatization of the company in question. The work collective has a right to decline the program it proposes twice, but the final decision rests with the local Soviet of People's Deputies. When an enterprise is transformed into a joint stock company, the procedure for the sale and distribution of stocks is defined by a property fund. When a company is auctioned, members of the work collective have a priority right of purchase.

Giving the work collective equal rights with the other would-be buyers is in line with market relations. Indeed, leaving social, psychological, and political motives aside, it makes economic sense to sell the property subject to privatization to the highest bidder. At first sight, this principle would boost the efficiency of reform and help attain the targets of privatization. But, although the economy should not be a means of dealing with political issues par excellence, neglect of social and political realities is also fraught with serious consequences.

First, such policy may produce a vast amount of litigation and, consequently, lengthen the time-terms of privatization and disrupt the normal production process. Second, at a certain stage forced privatization could provoke an outburst of indignation on the part of large population groups. Third, "outside" prospective buyers should not be idealized. In most cases these are not civilized businessmen ready to raise the standard of production and fill the market with goods. As a rule, persons wishing to buy property pursue entirely different goals: invest their money and thus avoid losing it to inflation, to launder "shadow" money, to sell the property at a profit or lease it, etc. As a result of such privatization, genuine producers are left with just nothing.

I believe the right way would be:

- in most cases, to consider the interests of work collectives in the greatest possible measure;
- to launch a large-scale popularization campaign refraining from severing the Gordian knot formed by fear of the mafia and failure to understand the essence of a market economy;
- whenever necessary, to use economic, not administrative coercion.

Enterprises and companies can and should be propelled towards privatization with the help of economic levers, to do which, all state-owned companies (except those on the not-to-be-privatized list) should be leased on an obligatory basis, with the funds subsequently created with the profits left at the disposal of the company regarded as share property of the work collective.

WAYS OF ACCOMPLISHING REFORM

The laws of Russia and a number of other republics do not identify the forms of de-etatization: lease without right of purchase, transformation into a public joint-stock company, the purchase of property subject to privatization by state-owned enterprises and companies, etc. Neither do they single out such form of privatization as the purchase of the company by its staff and establishment of a collective enterprise. Purchase through lease is limited.

Why has *collective enterprise* been excluded from the list of privatization forms? It has been proved that combining the functions of owner and hired laborer, that is, setting up collective enterprises, results in lower economic efficiency as compared to private or joint-stock companies. Furthermore, in many instances the transformation of a state into a collective enterprise signifies the victory of group interests over those of society at large. This is probably the reason why the Russian law restricts the use of this form of privatization.

As the experience of collective enterprises shows, the most complicated problem arising in the course of privatization is the form of collective ownership. Should it be shared, personified, or indivisible?

In my view, rejection of personification makes it impossible to reach the goals of privatization fully, specifically, does nothing to help the co-owners-cum-employees develop the "owner's feeling". Of course, it is far less trouble not to divide the property and purchase it using profits, gradually dividing the increment part of registered capital among the employees' shares commensurately with their labor contribution. In this case its share would be minuscule.

Neither does the Russian law make it easy to purchase leased property, which could be another form of privatization. This is allowed only when:

- when the contract on the lease with subsequent right of purchase had been signed before the law came into force;
- when the lessee obtains the right to purchase property subject to privatization on a competitive basis or through auction.

The law also establishes that the rent cannot be set off against the cost of the assets, which often makes purchase through lease too expensive.

The most popular privatization form will probably be auctioning, which makes it possible

- to change the form of ownership of large enterprises and companies with costly assets;
- to pave the way for new methods and organizational forms of sectoral management;
- to preserve economic links;
- to attract capital (including foreign capital) to update, re-equip, and expand production.

But auctioning does not remedy the workers' alienation from ownership of the means of production and may serve to disperse assets. What is even worse, under this form of privatization a significant block of shares may go to the state, giving it a chance to interfere into management. To remove this threat, the Russian law establishes that out of the number of shares of any joint-stock company owned by the property fund on behalf of the state, the right of vote may belong to not more than 20%, while the rest become preference stock. However, in some cases the rights of the state as proprietor should not be curtailed to this extent, since some companies could be transformed into joint-stock ones only if the state retains control over their operation.

THE COMPETITION AND THE AUCTION

The fact that these forms are interchangeable makes one think about the criteria of the choice. The auction has an advantage in that it provides an opportunity to derive maximum profits, that the winner is there for everyone to see, and that there is little chance of transgressions. The competition provides a comprehensive picture when the winner is determined and makes it possible to keep track of the future of the privatized company. The choice of the form of sale depends on the type and importance of the company or enterprise in question.

At the moment, the most current form of "minor privatization" is the auction.

Mistakes in this matter are frequent and serious. The first and most dangerous one is incompetent valuation. The proportion of "accurate hits", when the offered and the purchase price coincide, is only 10-20%. In the rest of the cases the lot is either over- or under priced.

Due to carelessness in the auction procedure and the vagueness of legal regulation, many lots are usually withdrawn from auctioning because there are no bidders, or several and even all lots are bought up by one person. Is it sensible to create new monopolists with one hand while undermining the monopoly of the state with the other?

In many instances the bodies empowered to conduct privatization would do well to use the services of more seasoned dealers: exchanges, banks, commercial funds. Capitalizing on the fact that the newly-hatched organizers of privatization are only learning market rules, commercial bodies buy cheap at auctions today so as to sell at market prices tomorrow.

So far, not a single goal of privatization has been attained. The several dozen large or medium-sized companies (such as Moven or KAMAZ) privatized in the full sense of the term (they should not be mixed up with a vast number of so-called joint-stock companies, concerns, and associations that merely disguise the former ministries and sectoral administrative departments) cannot salvage the economy on the national scale. Even total privatization of retail trade, the communal services, and public catering would fail to do this either. To build a free market, we need large-scale privatization in all branches of the national economy. But reform of this magnitude must rest on a firm legal basis, or the progress of privatization will lead only to extended reproduction of chaos and lawlessness.

The Non-State Sector In The Russian Economic System

T.Kuznetsova, Cand.Sc. (Econ.)
Institute of Economics, Russian Academy of Sciences

The Role and Place of the Non-State Sector under the Totalitarian Regime

As the totalitarian economic system is dismantled, the role and place of the non-state sector will have to change. The chosen strategy and the evolution of this sector generally and its various components in particular will determine many significant economic relations and links. First, the short-term development policy of the non-state sector will set the rates and conditions of transition to the free market. Second, the scope of the inter-regional market will depend on the legal principles of the functioning of the non-state sector in the various regions. Third, the restrictions imposed on the development of this sector in the various economic spheres will determine how and to what extent the production and social potential of the territories and regions will be used. Fourth, overall economic efficiency, including that of the state sector, will depend on whether certain economic forms will be banned or permitted in the non-state sector. Fifth, the functioning of the non-state networks as an economic sector with single economic principles, a market economic mechanism, and single bodies of legal and social principles will determine the conditions and factors enabling the state to drastically change its functions to adapt to the transition to new economic relations.

A non-state sector can be established both by setting up new non-state enterprises and by privatization, that is, transforming state-run economic units into non-state or mixed ones.

The non-state sector has a long history in this country. It was shaped within the framework of the totalitarian regime, fulfilled a certain function, and had a place, features, and scope of its own. Paradoxically enough, in a state-run and owned administrative central system, which should have, it seems, found it easier and more logical to reduce all economic systems to a uniform hierarchy, the non-state sector managed to survive. Since wholesale collectivization of agriculture, when an economic mechanism severely regimenting all economic processes was built, the country had quite a substantial non-state sector both as regards the number of people engaged in it, the scope of production, and the influence on the economy.

For years, the non-state sector included a considerable part of the economy, connected chiefly with the sphere of consumption. Officially it was represented by the collective farms and individual subsidiary holdings, that is, the chief producers of food; producer cooperatives, which accounted for about 6% of industrial output (mainly consumer goods: up to 40% of furniture, 35% of knitwear, 70% of metal dishes, etc.) and the bulk of communal services; consumer cooperatives, which manufactured consumer goods from agricultural raw materials and acted as trade intermediaries between agriculture and industry, the rural and the urban areas; small private businesses; and subsidiary production and services. Official statistics say that licensed non-state sector engaged over 25 million average annual workers, that is, at least 25% of the overall number of employees in the national economy (late 1950s-early 1960s).

A large share of the non-state sector was constituted by unlicensed forms of economic activity conducted by individuals (building and servicing private housing, repairs of all kinds, clothes-making).

One can safely say that in the mid-1960s, nearly all consumption of the rural and a large share of urban population was ensured by the non-state sector.

Until the late 1950s-early 1960s, the non-state sector had played a fateful role in our economy. Embracing collective-farm production and the subsidiary businesses, consumer and producer cooperatives, and individual subsidiary holdings, it supplied the consumer market and fed the bulk of the population (naturally, as best it could and no better than the country at large was fed), thus consolidating the totalitarian system. Its employees were viewed not as producers of goods society needed but as profiteers, recipients of unearned incomes, etc., with all ensuing consequences. This view has not changed much.

Very early on, a relentless campaign was launched to replace or oust the non-state sector by networks operating on behalf of the totalitarian state. In the 1950s, producer cooperatives were abolished, and in the 1960s, collective farms were transformed into state-run ones and consumer cooperatives began to turn into a clumsy bureaucratic system servicing mainly the interests of the steadily growing apparatus and not the people who had set them up and were maintaining them.

The rapid growth of production in 1953-1958 and its subsequent decline probably occurred because the non-state sector first expanded and then was drastically curtailed. What is more, it is clear in retrospect that in the late 1960s, the urgent need for reform stemmed also from the continued contraction of the state sector. But the latter's "improvement" did not entail any really significant changes.

Each step taken to undermine the non-state sector weakened the centralized command system, which was obliged to look for replacements for the non-state sector inside the system itself. But as this was impossible, either the non-state sector was allowed to breath a little more easily, or the screws were turned even tighter.

Like the elimination of the peasantry during wholesale collectivization, the abolition of producer cooperatives showed yet again that the non-state sector cannot be replaced. The campaign to do away with producer cooperatives, which meant greater economic unification, naturally became an effort to strengthen monopoly not only in the production of capital goods but also in the manufacture of consumer goods and the communal services, and a campaign (bordering on gigantomania) to increase the size of enterprises and to excessively strengthen the sectoral principles of economic management.

Until recently, economic advancement was expected to rest on two principles, a single form of ownership and large-scale production. In practical terms this meant turning collective into state-run farms, curtailing small private farming, prohibiting farmers to own cattle, and cutting down the number of enterprises by making them larger.

As a result of the pressure put on small private farming, agricultural output declined, and a number of administrative bans on the non-state sector had to be lifted. But the overall trend towards its abolition continued to determine economic policy.

Neither did the non-state sector fit in very well with "developed socialism". But, as the economy was unable to function without it, there was a certain amount of legal private activity, as well as a fair amount of unlicensed private business.

THE STRUCTURE OF NON-STATE BUSINESS UNDER ADMINISTRATIVE DIKTAT

By the degree of "etatization", the non-state sector fell into two categories. The first comprised the farms and enterprises under immediately influence of the totalitarian system. The second bowed to the system and experienced some pressure from it but enjoyed some freedom of action. The first embraced public economic forms - collective farms and consumer and producer cooperatives, and the second - non-public forms: individual subsidiary holdings and all private business that was either not officially licensed or directly banned. Formally, the first employed about two-thirds, and the second - one-third of the personnel working in the not-state sector. But, in actual fact, everyone in the country had some dealings with unofficial private business. The private segment of the non-state sector was always more efficient than the public, and, of course, more efficient than the state sector, although the bulk of resources was channelled into the latter. The non-state sector and especially its private segment had elements of market relations, such as equivalent exchange, specialization of production, and rational division of labor.

THE ENVIRONMENT OF THE FUNCTIONING OF THE NON-STATE SECTOR

Aware of the significance of the non-state sector, having extended the legal framework of its operation and licensed new economic forms, the state continues its economic blockade (in the choice of spheres of operation and access to material and other resources). But as the issues of de-etatization of economic relations, privatization, and the shaping of a mixed economy were arose and were resolved, the expansion, consolidation, and advancement of the non-state sector is becoming irreversible. However, for it to live up to its potential, a favorable environment is necessary. First, we must discard the ideological bias against both the non-state sector and the possibility of building a mixed economy. This bias is still strong. Ideology is affecting not only the concrete conditions of the establishment of non-state businesses but also leads to certain state decisions (resolution on prohibited types of cooperative work, official non-recognition of private ownership in resources). Second, we must finally recognize how important the non-state sector is for the transition to the free market. Obviously, the market is essential for the non-state sector to realize its essential characteristics. In its turn, the market can be established only if the non-state sector is promoted, monopoly combated, competition encouraged, etc. Third, we should proceed from the fact that a developed non-state sector can alone enable the state sector to make the best possible use of its advantages. Fourth, the economy as a whole can function efficiently only if it leaves room for a multitude of economic forms and allows the state and the non-state sector to develop dynamically, interact, and intertwine.

To pave the way for the non-state sector, it is important not to try to set its boundaries "from above". They must be established naturally, on the basis of economic and social expediency, the interests of individuals and industries. Expansion of its scope stimulates economic de-etatization.

The non-state sector may extend to any sphere or branch of the economy. There should be no principle restrictions here. But at the time of transition to the free market, the priorities of its development should be identified correctly. At the moment, they include the manufacture of agricultural produce, its processing and storage, all light industry branches, all kinds of repairs, the manufacture of spare parts, all types of social and communal services, a more efficient use of our intellectual potential, and the use of locally available raw materials.

It is important to identify the enterprises and production and service spheres that are ready to go over from the state to the non-state sector. Second, the state sector itself contains parts that would be easy to withdraw from state control (collective farms, consumer cooperatives). Third, state-run enterprises whose efficiency can be raised by transferring them to the non-state sector should be prepared to make the transition by advancing commercialization. Fourth, new enterprises should be allowed to choose whether to work within the state or the non-state sector. And, finally, the stress on the priorities must not hamper the other, currently non-priority spheres. Long-term prospects should also be considered.

THE SCOPE AND STRUCTURE OF THE NASCENT NON-STATE SECTOR

It is not too difficult to define them formally But figures do not always give an accurate idea of the development trends in the non-state sector. The difficulty lies mainly in the fact that in a number of cases, state and non-state enterprises and companies merge, non-state companies resort to mimicry, pass themselves as state-run ones, are forced to restrict and even conceal the sphere of their actual influence. For as long as many economic fields remain closed to them, they will be obliged to wage a semi-legal, shadow existence. And this makes it impossible to determine the real scope of the state and the non-state sectors and, consequently, the scale of forthcoming privatization. This is a feature of all ex-Union republics.

When de-etatization and privatization were declared, many state (including sectoral, structural) enterprises and companies began to imitate non-state and "semi-state" associations, concerns, consortiums, and joint-stock companies. By itself, the merger of state and non-state establishments is not an evil when there is a normal market environment, commercialization equally involves all economic structures, entrepreneurship advances, all economic forms are ensured equal conditions as a matter of principle, and not a single one is legally granted significant advantages. In our economy, such equality is non-existent. Market, commercial, or, to use a fashionable word, alternative and, in actual fact, non-state structures legally possess more economic freedom but do not have the material and financial resources or the "command heights" at the disposal of the state structures, which, however, do not have economic freedom. As a result, the economy is making no headway and the "marriage" of state and non-state companies enables them to use the advantages of both and leads to corruption and the loss or concealment of the economic potential of both, obstructing the movement to civilized market relations. As of January 1, 1991, operating in the country were 126 concerns, 1,420 associations, 102 consortiums, and 1,259 joint-stock companies, although the economic mechanism has not changed noticeably. What is more, in the sphere of production new non-state bodies are practically non-existent, with the exception of a number of cooperatives and joint ventures, private farms, and self-employed persons. The new economic forms are incorporated into what is known as the market infrastructure, but without production of goods the latter is not worth much. This has become quite clear over the past few years. All kinds of exchanges, broker's offices, and other middleman organizations are mushrooming, while in production nothing is happening. A large number of exchanges is engaged mainly in selling the accumulated stockpiles of raw materials and imported goods. The prices in nearly all transactions are grossly inflated. The volume and scale of transactions are not large. This shows, first, that there is not enough goods at the exchanges, and, second, that street-market deals are common. What is more, only about 20% of the goods sold at the exchanges is purchased directly by consumers, while the bulk is bought to be resold.

The new private infrastructure is far too weakly linked with production and is doing nothing to restructure it. Furthermore, varied and often ownerless resources on vast territories enable a large segment of this infrastructure to lead a parasitic existence capitalizing on the lack of consistency in economic tactic and strategy and the weakness of local executive and legislative authority.

A way out of this situation may be offered by privatization provided that it is really given green light and not restricted to a few spheres and types of enterprise and company.

A truly vital issue for the future of the private sector is privatization of natural resources (land, forests, etc.). So far, privatization has been mentioned only in connection with land and agricultural production, but very soon this will not be enough. Large-scale privatization is bound to raise the issue of ownership of all resources, and we must anticipate this by devising privatization mechanisms that would not leave the majority cheated once again and would make it clear who owns what.

THE FOOD CRISIS AND HOW TO GET OUT OF IT

Ivan Buzdalov, D.Sc. (Econ.)
Russian Agricultural Academy

Several signs enable one to talk about crisis in agriculture: the production slump, especially in the manufacture of marketable goods; lower efficiency of investments; the ageing of the population employed in agriculture; desolation of large areas in Russia while others have large redundant human resources; the deteriorating ecological situation, large-scale degeneration of land; the overall psychological situation in rural areas, general disillusionment in the collective- and state-farm system; absence of a favorable material, technical, and economic environment for the development of private farming, rejection of private enterprise and new forms of cooperation in the countryside; a backward social infrastructure there.

Pent-up demand for food already amounts to 45-50 billion roubles. The food shortages are caused, not so much by the low level of production as by the losses of produce during harvesting, storage, transportation, and processing. There is also the trend towards lower inputs into agriculture and the growing prices for machinery, fertilizers, etc.

Trade being in total disarray, the food prices are growing much faster than most people's incomes, and this is worsening the social and economic situation and obstructing ecological reform and a transition to market relations.

Overcoming the crisis is made difficult by the irreversible or hard-to-reverse changes in the agricultural sector, especially in natural and human resources. The most general significant barrier in the way out of the crisis is the absence of an efficient mechanism of market relations. Neither is there a clear science-based concept of such a mechanism that would work in a situation when the ex-Soviet Union is ceasing to function and new principles of economic cooperation among the newly-sovereign states have not yet been defined.

At the moment, the main problem is to provide a sound foundation for the new principles and the very mechanism of increasing food supplies and rationally distributing what is available in the crisis situation. Not only production but distribution of food should begin using economic methods and incentives and market principles, although non-market food funds for a strictly defined category of people in the low income bracket should also be set up.

Only radical agrarian reform and a resolute transition to the free market can get the country out of the cul-de-sac in which Russian agriculture has found itself both economically and socially.

The food shortages can be alleviated as early as 1992 if the state arranges an exchange of agricultural machinery and equipment, building materials, and consumer goods for agricultural produce using agreed prices and barter, ensures that the losses of food are cut down (e.g., by building more storage space directly where it is produced), and resorts to large-scale import and technical and other assistance from abroad.

These are mainly one-time measures requiring administrative interference into production processes and the system of distribution of food. The strategic goals are building a free market, privatization, introduction of private ownership of land, freedom of enterprise and trade, and unimpeded development of the markets of labor, capitals, and land.

These are all problems facing not only agriculture but the economy as a whole, which urgently needs healthier finances, money circulation, and a convertible rouble. To effect radical economic reform in agriculture, it is vitally important that the ex-republics sign agreements on mutual deliveries and payments in the so-called agro-industrial complex.

At present, when executive authority has been weakened, debates have replaced action, economic reforms are half-hearted, and agrarian laws are not working, it is necessary to work out a single concept or program of agrarian reform and to give it all the legal props it needs. This is a necessary initial stage of agrarian reform.

The Chief Elements of Land Reform

The Russian land law and the laws of the other ex-republics need to be revised and amended: (1) it should be permitted to sell agricultural land not only to the state but to private persons, and to lease it for agricultural use to foreign citizens; (2) owners of land should be permitted to sell it after not more than five years of ownership; (3) land banks and courts should be set up and other conditions provided for the functioning of land markets, provided that the standards of rational land use are met; (4) it should be permitted to use hired labor, with employees of all types of farms having equal social guarantees.

We need a differentiated approach to the privatization of land and the other means of production. Bankrupt farms and agricultural companies must be privatized in full and transferred to new private owners or cooperatives. The state should help private farms to purchase materials and equipment and sell their produce, and develop the production and social infrastructure and various types of non-agricultural activities. The rest of state-run and collective farms, which are competitive and account for about 70% of agricultural produce, should be reconstructed on the principles of cooperation and self-government, becoming joint-stock companies or associations.

To give owners of land more reliable legal protection, farmers' unions should be set up by delegating representatives of agricultural commodity producers. The union's representative bodies in the center and the provinces in collaboration with the land authorities should directly participate in drafting new agrarian laws and have a right to control their observance, up to revoking decisions of local authorities and work collectives.

The drafting and implementation of land reform designed to make land the property of natural and legal persons would, of course, help reconstruct the social and economic system of agriculture.

Combating the Agrarian Crisis

The state's agricultural policies should begin using economic management methods. The new relations should rest on a system of equal treaties; monopoly in the supplies, sales and price-formation must be dismantled. No time should be lost taking steps to improve the storage, transportation, and procession of agricultural produce if the losses, and, correspondingly, food imports, are to be reduced. Out of the 70 billion roubles in investments in the agro-industrial complex, less than 15% is used to help cut down the losses on the way of food from producer to consumer. This sum should be at least doubled (e.g., by revising the structure of imports).

Outside contacts in this sphere should be rechannelled from the import of food to that of equipment, machinery, and technologies, the training of farmers and, generally, a new type of farmer-entrepreneur, and finding a niche in the world market of agricultural produce. In 1992, when the crisis is expected to reach its peak, imported foodstuffs should be used as sensibly as possible. Export-import operations should be given financial privileges.

The overall market concept of agrarian reform makes it necessary to revise the procedure of the purchase of agricultural produce. Considering that administrative methods are no longer able to make producers meet state orders (tax in kind), direct contracts should be used to buy goods from producers. With this end in view, the network of state-run purchase organizations should be demonopolized, and competition from consumer cooperatives, markets and other types of wholesale trade should be encouraged.

The food bought by the state bodies should be sold through the retail trade network and delivered on orders from enterprises and companies, with the exception of the foodstuffs going to the centralized reserve fund and to the army and other "special" clients. The distribution of food should be monitored by republican bodies.

To minimize the risk run by private entrepreneurs and protect low earners, a fund of inter-state support for the agrarian sector should be set up on agreement of the members of the economic community. This fund can be used to index purchase prices for the agricultural produce to meet the growth of prices for agricultural machinery, equipment, fertilizers, and services, and to maintain fixed wholesale prices for the products of the food and the manufacturing industries should purchase prices for agricultural raw materials go up. Some money from this fund could be used to keep up the incomes of agricultural producers hit by natural calamities.

Until food shortages have eased, the profits of all enterprises and companies in the agro-industrial complex should be taxed on preferential terms.

To carry out social programs in the countryside, a more efficient and purposeful use should be made of the money given by local budgets and voluntary purposeful allocations by enterprises.

Reforming the agrarian sector on the basis of these principles and practical suggestions implies drafting a whole new agrarian law. Without a legal base which would be able to abolish all obstacles in the way of free enterprise, radical reform of the agrarian sector would again be indefinitely delayed. And this would amount to a national tragedy.

The State and the Prospects of the Russian Food Industry

Rustam Gumerov, Can.Sc.(Econ.)
Institute of Economic Research,
Economic Ministry of the Russian Federation

The Anatomy of the Crisis

In 1990-1991, the crisis of the food industry in Russia and the Soviet Union generally manifested itself in a production decline that became a stable tendency; lower volume of purchases; disrupted food supplies due to non-observance of the schedule of deliveries to the centralized fund, and a large number of new customs restrictions.

These adverse trends were generated, above all, by the collapse of the system of centralized inputs into agriculture, as a result of which the state lost a powerful lever of influence upon agricultural producers. One of the consequences was that the systems of obligatory sale and purchase and agricultural supplies stopped working, while an alternative network was non-existent.

In 1990-1991, agriculture began to feel the pressure of prices. In the first half of 1991, the index of prices for industrial goods supplied to agriculture was 183% as compared to the same period of 1990, while the index of prices for agricultural produce (along all sales channels) was only 156%.

Attempts to retaliate were futile and only aggravated the situation in the food market. In the absence of a commodity equivalent of their produce, collective and state-run farms chose the well-known behavioral model and tried to attain relative financial stability by inflating prices and reducing sales. This trend first manifested itself back in 1990, after agreed prices for potatoes, vegetables, and fruits had been introduced. The average potato prices rose (as compared to 1989) 1.3 times, and vegetable prices - 1.5 times. The revenues from their sales increased by 8.5 billion roubles, but the production of potatoes on nearly all types of farms dropped by almost 12% and of vegetables - by 8%, while the volume of purchase declined by 25% and 13% respectively.

Another aspect of the food crisis is the extreme backwardness of the sales, transportation, processing and storage of agricultural produce and raw materials. It is not so much the high losses of produce (incidentally, foreign, e.g., British experts estimate them, not at 20-30% but at about 10% of the produce, with the rest falling to "underharvesting" due to the low technological level of Russian agriculture) as the organizational principles of this section of the agro-industrial complex, its monopolistic structure. This problem cannot be resolved by simply rechannelling some of the money into its "third link".

The state-run agricultural produce-delivery network is a monopolist largely because the other sales channels are underdeveloped. In 1991, the state-run network of the ex-Soviet Union accounted for the bulk of the produce purchased from agricultural enterprises, which was distributed and redistributed through a multi-tiered, hard-to-manage and control state trade network. Falling to the other sales outlets (consumer cooperatives, the so-called collective-farm market, private shops) was between one and four percent.

There is reason to believe that the adverse trends of 1990-1991 will also make themselves felt and may even become stronger in 1992 and 1993. Despite the more or less adequate preparations for the 1992 grain harvest (in October, winter crops occupied 19.9 million hectares as compared to 16.5 million hectares in the previous year, and the autumn ploughed area intended for spring sowing - 56 million as against 44 million hectares), at the time of principal agricultural works the rural areas will feel a shortage of pesticides, fuel, and machinery.

Collective and state-run farms can be expected to reduce the areas under the more labor-intensive crops, beetroot, vegetables, potatoes. The reason is a shortage of harvesting equipment and scarcity of labor during the harvesting season.

The necessary state food funds can most probably be set up on the basis of the President's decision of January 4, 1992 on obligatory deliveries of agricultural produce. But the decision has, in principle, an anti-market character and may do some good only in the next one or two years; this means that other measures will have to be mapped out to make agricultural production more marketable.

LOOKING FOR WAYS OUT OF THE CRISIS

The need for agrarian reform is self-evident, as is the fact that its principal component will be a land reform designed to pave the way for economic diversity in agriculture and give the various types of farms and other agricultural enterprises equal opportunities for advancement. However, theoretical debates and the practical work of executive bodies tend to distort the essence of land reform and turn it into an end in itself. The first changes were lopsided, overstressing as they did the establishment of private or family farms. The growth in the latter's number is supposed to indicate how successful land reform is, and supposed "indisputable advantages" of private farming have supplied it with an ideological background.

There are some basic factors. First, in the industrialized countries agriculture functions as an integral system of large, medium-sized, and small farms and enterprises in different forms of ownership; having a place of its own, neither type of production unit has advantages over the others. Second, the stake at private interest and labor motivation is justified only inasmuch as they can be put to practical "use". Third, any change in the social and economic structure of the agrarian sector is bound to take time; in the interim, transitional economic forms employing efficient state regulation methods should be used. Fourth, land reform would yield no results if unaccompanied by a corresponding revision of the systems of material and technical supplies and sales of agricultural produce.

To prove that private farms have an edge over the existing state-run and collective ones, individual subsidiary holdings (in which similar labor motivations operate) are often cited as a model of efficiency. Indeed, their contribution to food production is large enough: the State Committee for Statistics says that in 1990, they accounted for slightly more than 25% of gross agricultural output. A "head-on" comparison seems to indicate that such holdings indeed have absolute advantages over large collective farms. But some figures belie this conclusion.

First, the share of individual subsidiary holdings in the production of some agricultural crops roughly corresponds to their share in the overall area under these crops.

Second, "private" livestock and poultry is fed mainly with fodder produced on public land. According to some estimates, at least 80 million hectares of public land is used for this purpose.

Third, the high share of individual holdings in the overall volume of agricultural output is largely determined by their concentration on more profitable crops (central planning and price-formation rob collective and state-run farms of a chance to do the same).

Individual holdings are a production form that closely interacts with the collective forms on the basis of specialization and cooperation.

Large farms (modern state-run and collective farms) can find a place for themselves in the free market in a certain environment.

Practically all industrialized countries use lease/hire of land. In the USA, about 43%, and in Holland, 35% of agricultural land is not owned but rented. What is more, everywhere the state encourages the purchase of land by the direct producer, the lessee, and in most states sub-lease is also possible. In a modern economy, lease/hire is a natural form of market self-regulation of the size of plots in use.

Are Current Forecasts of the Future of Private Farming Accurate?

Once given the green light, private farms in Russia began to spring up rapidly enough. According to the Russian minister for agriculture and food, by late 1991-early 1992, the number of private farms reached about 50,000. Without question, being a new economic form, the establishment of private/family farms must be subject to special control; it is equally obvious that an attempt should be made to forecast the evolution of this process.

The first steps of private farming in Russia show that it is facing the same problems (which have produced the present crisis) as collective and state-run farming. The Committee for Statistics says that in 1991, their share in gross agricultural output was about 1%, which corresponds to the area on which they are working. As of July 1, 1991, for each hundred private farms there were 47 tractors, 14 trucks, five combine harvesters, 17 ploughs, 12 sowing machines, nine machine scythes, three reaping machines, and three pick-up harvesters.

An inspection of private farms registered by June 1, 1991 showed that less than one-third (27.7%) of them were set up by persons who had left collective or state-run farms. The new farmers were mostly people who had not been working in agriculture immediately before their venture, and this makes one doubt the stability and marketability prospects of private farming in its present form. A large share of registered farmers are likely to go bankrupt (the Baltics have already confirmed this), their debts will be written off, and productive agricultural land will go out of economic and commodity turnover.

WHAT IS TO BE DONE?

Land reform should be considered more carefully; the trends accompanying it should be monitored, and more account should be taken of the concrete objective conditions of its realization.

The chief lesson the present situation has taught us is that the market self-regulation mechanism should not prevent the state from doing what it can to make the production and distribution of food efficient. During the transition period, state regulation of food production has the following main functions:

1. Budget financing of comprehensive programs along the priority trends of food production, such as restoring fertility of the soil and building up the agrarian infrastructure.

2. A vigorous taxation policy. To relieve the tension in the consumer market, foodstuffs along the entire "agricultural raw materials-foodstuffs sold through the retail outlets" chain should be exempt from VAT.

To make up what the budget would lose, at least in part, the rate of land tax, which was established prior to price liberalization, should be raised. However, the chief idea behind this suggestion is to make agricultural production more marketable and to oust the landowners and land users who regard land as mainly a good investment.

3. Forming and using state food funds, elaborating a mechanism of voluntary participation of the reorganized collective and state-run farms and private farms' in the effort to shape state-owned food reserves. The most efficient method would be to protect

agricultural producers against the diktat of monopoly producers of resources for agriculture. This can be done by, first, introducing state-guaranteed supplies using deliveries of agricultural produce as warranty. To find the necessary resources, industrial enterprises should be granted extensive taxation privileges. Second, the prices for the produce of agricultural enterprises taking part in supplying the state food funds on contract basis should be indexed to the growing prices for manufactured goods.

4. Promoting the development of multi-channel material and technical supplies and sales of agricultural produce and taking anti-monopoly steps in this field. Using a variety of levers (credit and taxation policies), the state should make it a priority to promote a diversified network of enterprises processing, storing, and selling agricultural produce (farmers' cooperatives, own wholesale and retail outlets, direct contacts, etc.).

5. Control over the commodity markets. There should be a differentiated approach to the study and regulation of the markets dealing in individual types of agricultural produce. Their specific problems should be dealt with on the basis of sectoral programs, bearing in mind that different sectors will behave differently during land reform, price liberalization, and revision of the commodity-producing network, and that each commodity market will encounter obstacles that will be unlike any others. Such programs will make it possible to support certain categories of farms and agricultural enterprises, both reorganized large public, and medium-sized and small ones. This approach would be much more efficient than automatic formal support of private farming.

Crisis As An Economic Instrument. Energy Consumption Will Go Down

Inna Gritsevich
Commission for the Study of
Productive Forces and Natural Resources
Russian Academy of Sciences

The Fuel Crisis and Its Trends

In late 1991 the fuel and energy crisis acquired a new dimension: brief local interruptions of supply became permanent and at times reached a national scale, disrupting normal functioning of whole large regions. The slump affected not only the production of oil and coal, which was 6.1% and 5% respectively in 1990 and 10% and 11% in 1991, but also the mining of gas, which first began to fall in the end of 1991. Officials in the coal industry are predicting a shortage of 40 million tons of coal in 1992. The decline of oil production cannot be stopped either. Energy supplies are going to deteriorate even further.

The Level and Structure of Energy Consumption: Comparative Assessments

This turn of events is not at all unexpected. Long before the state-run economic system fell apart, experts had been warning that the old energy strategy outlived itself, was putting a growing strain on the natural environment and the economy, and would result in an energy crisis. The situation throughout the Commonwealth of Independent States has since become critical.

In the meantime, it is well known that the ex-USSR and now the Commonwealth is holding one of the first places in the world in primary per capita energy consumption (not true of the other essential goods and services). Ahead of it are economically prosperous but very northern countries (Canada, Sweden, and Norway), the wasteful United States, and Australia with its mighty mining industry. The power capacity of the national economy per unit of GNP is also too high.

A Western study comparing the patterns of energy consumption in the Soviet Union with market economies which resemble it in the principal objective conditions (climate, availability of energy resources, economic structure) revealed huge overconsumption of energy. By some estimates, by the end of the 1980s, the Soviet economy consumed roughly twice as much energy per unit of end product than the OECD countries. More sophisticated evaluation methods show that the overconsumption rooted in the features of the economic system reached 60% of overall energy consumption.

Also peculiar to the USSR was the structure of energy consumption, in which human needs were least important: over a half of the energy is used up by industry, which is much more than in any industrialized country, while only 15.9% fall to the share of the municipality. A significant but difficult-to-measure share is used by the military-industrial complex. The officially recognized fact that military spending equals about 30% of GNP means that the military-industrial complex consume no less than 30% of the energy (probably more), considering that the manufacture of military equipment and armaments and their functioning have an extra-high power capacity, as well as the fact that the state has never stinted the military-industrial complex of energy and other resources and that the latter was not subject to ecological control. Furthermore, due to the same factors the military-industrial complex is indirectly affecting the power capacity of the economy generally, creating a large additional demand for the produce of energy-intensive civilian industries (metallurgy, the fuel branches).

ENERGY-SAVING OPPORTUNITIES

There also exist assessments of technological energy-saving opportunities which could be used in the next few years. They are extensive enough to save significant amounts of fuel, help reduce pollution, lighten the anthropogenic greenhouse effect, and slow down climatic changes. In medium term, energy consumption could be cut down by 30% through obvious technical and economic steps alone. According to quite realistic estimates, annual energy consumption could be reduced by 220 million tons in terms of oil, the amount consumed by Great Britain or the whole of Africa.

ENERGY-SAVING FACTORS AND METHODS

Obviously, energy-saving opportunities will not realize themselves. In the industrialized countries, where after the energy crisis of the 1970s a virtual energy-saving revolution took place, the decisive role belonged to market mechanisms, which were more or less successfully boosted by state policies. The source of the revolution was a more efficient use of energy in all aspects of society's life as a result of technological, structural, and behavioral shifts.

The situation which exists and is likely to continue for some time in Russia and the other Commonwealth states also leaves room for a version of energy-saving, albeit a different one. It will not be a consequence of a more efficient use of energy in the national economy stemming from a purposeful state policy, but will made possible by the dismantling of the old political and economic system and the transition to the free market.

In the Commonwealth of Independent States, an important factor of energy saving interpreted in the broad sense as energy consumption below a certain earlier level is the decline in the production of practically all energy resources. In 1991 Russia, for instance, produced 11% less of coal and oil than in 1990 (bigger drop than in GNP generally). Considering that the country has neither the capital nor the technologies required to maintain the production of energy resources, the slump is likely to continue.

Another equally important reason why energy consumption is bound to go down is the production decline in most industries due to the collapse of the old social, economic, and political system (in Russia, it fell by 9% of GNP in 1991). The worst hit was metallurgy, which produced 18%, 14%, and 13% less of pig iron, steel, and rolled steel respectively. Production, especially in the basic industries, can be expected to fall even further in the next two or three years and reach 25-40% of the 1989 level. The sharply rising energy prices and withdrawal of budget support for enterprises will further reduce the demand for the goods of most basic industries forcing them to fold up production, which will decline 1.2-1.5 times more than in the economy generally.

If the government of Russia decides to launch privatization and will demilitarize the economy further, structural economic reform will also become a factor of energy saving. If subsidies for the industries whose share should rise are not forthcoming, the process will have to proceed through an even greater production drop in the industries whose share is too high by market standards, and most of them consume a lot of energy. The latter's consumption will correspondingly fall in the sphere of material production as a whole.

Economic disintegration in the Commonwealth and in Russia in particular will hardly stop in 1991 but is likely to continue over the next two or three years at least. Decline and stagnation will persist especially in large-scale industry, especially in its basic branches: under the currently planned programs they are not to be subject to privatization for a long time to come, which will also obstruct de-etatization of the production of consumer goods and services increasing unemployment and underemployment and conserving a low living standard and purchasing power of the bulk of the population, and, in consequences, reducing the demand for goods and services.

Small-scale privatization, which is planned for the first stage of transition to market relations, has little significance in relation to energy consumption, since the communal services are not using much anyway. Private farming will also be labor-intensive at the first stage of its development and will not really change the economy's energy capacity.

As a result of the production slump, real incomes and the living standard of large population groups have plummeted: on average, they may go back to the level of the mid-1950s. The wealth gap is bound to widen. People will use less energy.

Over the transition period, the more important factors will be the ones reducing energy consumption and the economy's power capacity proportionately to the decline of production and the living standard. The final outcome of disintegration and transition may prove more significant than using technological energy-saving opportunities.

The extracting industries are an integral part of the economic system and cannot be set aside as a separate economic zone, an oasis of healthy market economy. Even if they are adequately supplied with capital goods, society will be unable to make a good use of their produce. It may therefore be for the best that not only the consumption but also the production of energy resources is going down: this will save their reserves until better times.

THE "SHADOW" PART OF THE SOVIET BUREAUCRATIC ICEBERG

Alexander Bunich, Cand.Sc.(Econ.)

From the shadow economy and command system towards private ownership and the market - this is the Soviet way, at least for the present. As for the transition period, it was probably the time of the "hidden" or "shadow" economy.

The term "shadow economy" gained wide currency only in the early 1980s, when the first studies of this phenomenon were made and published by people working in the law-enforcement bodies and by "armchair" economists. Interest in this subject reached its peak in 1985-1990, probably owing to the notorious "cotton case".

By the early 1980s, the shadow economy presented an established network of relations among individuals and political, ethnic, and social groups inside the so-called command system, a network that operated on the basis of clearly defined principles. One may even say that "shadow relations" constituted the backbone of all interpersonal relations in the official hierarchy of the totalitarian Soviet state.

In principle, distinction between formal and non-formal power structures is typical not only of a long-established totalitarian bureaucratic state having a "shadow" side but of any management system. Experts in the theory of management note that in any system, the official hierarchy is only the tip of the iceberg, the chief, underwater part of which is constituted by non-formal structures. In the specifically Soviet environment, however, the non-formal management structure began to develop and function autonomously, gradually becoming highly corrupt and acquiring a mafia-like aspect. This blend of the non-formal and the mafia elements is what distinguishes the Soviet economic system from the others.

THE ROOTS OF THE SHADOW ECONOMY

There is reason to believe that illegal wealth under socialism has deep roots, which first became visible in the 1950s. The state, however, had contracted the virus of corruption much earlier. Back at the time of war communism, there already existed criminal groups which made a pile dealing in food and consumer essentials. Under the New Economic Policy (1920s), people who chose illegal ways to get rich were also numerous enough. The rigid Stalinist hierarchy did not make stealing impossible in the 1930s and even in the war years, when profiteers, second-hand dealers, and smugglers made fortunes, many of which found their way abroad together with their owners.

But, of course, the shadow economy boom fell to Brezhnev's epoch, when criminal groups mushroomed in virtually all regions of the country and in all industries. Occasionally, crusades against them was declared, but those were small-scale, local affairs. The official ideology permitted the existence of "isolated drawbacks", misdemeanors, and minor offenses. Now in the Caucasus, now in Moldavia, the Ukraine, or Central Asia, "isolated" criminal groups were exposed and punished. Thieves and bribe-takers were discovered now in light industry, now in retail trade, and now on the transport. By the late 1970s, it was already obvious that this type of crime could not be combated by such inefficient and outdated methods, and the law-enforcement bodies found themselves in the horns of a dilemma: either to arrest all economic executives, or to be satisfied with small fry.

There appeared mechanisms for re-pumping raw and other materials into the "shadow" sector, and state-run enterprises began to turn out produce that did not figure in their books. There were whole factories no one knew about (!) because their produce was "shadow". Projects that took decades to complete or were never completed and the notorious losses of produce in the agro-industrial complex served to enrich the mafia. Banks extended credits, the State Planning Committee approved construction projects, building materials were stolen, and the volume of accomplished construction was fraudulently overstated.

It would take a long time to describe all spheres in which shadow capital was used and the mechanisms of this operation. For instance, there appeared corrupt officials in the foreign trade network. It turned out that even deputy minister Sushkov took huge bribes for Soviet-Japanese contracts that were blatantly unfavorable for his own country. Thus, by the outset of the cotton case investigated by Gdlyan and Ivanov, the ground had already been knocked from under the feet of the law-enforcement bodies: corruption was everywhere.

THE BUREAUCRATIC MARKET

Sociologists and economists have discovered a so-called network of non-formal management interactions in the command system of "developed socialism". Some of them call it the "bureaucratic market". What does this mean?

Under centralized allocation of everything, rigid regimentation, and all-embracing planning, the economy could not have functioned if its agents did not enter into non-formal contacts with each other. Using status and influence, the various regions, enterprises, sectors, and even whole industries fought for lower plan targets, taxation privileges, cheap credits, subsidies, and investments. The strong devoured the weak. A system of tacit exchange of services was formed in production and distribution.

The theorists called all this the "bureaucratic market", arguing that not a single system, even a super-totalitarian one, can exist without market, if warped, relations.

THE ILLUSION OF LAW AND ORDER

Elderly people often say that under Stalin, corruption and stealing were non-existent, while now everyone is a crook. The Stalinist system did, indeed, make a great deal of trouble for the mafia.

The economic foundation of Stalinism did not need a shadow economy, and yet... Shadow economic processes begin at the bottom and grow and gain strength gradually, remaining invisible up to a certain point. Stalin did do away with profiteers and semi-criminal dealers, of whom the New Economic Policy produced not a few, but "in passing" he also destroyed millions (!) of honest, hard-working wealthy peasants, who would be called private farmers now, and "wreckers" in industry, now referred to as innovators and entrepreneurs. Even accepting this as normal, there is no guarantee that the seeds of harmful tendencies did not sprout later, when a favorable environment appeared.

First, the central planning bodies promptly lost all idea of what was really going on at the local level. Information was distorted systematically and deliberately to produce a good impression as factories and economic regions tried to win the notorious socialist competition. Second, in a centralized economy, the system of control gives the inspectors and the leaders' entourage an opportunity to engage in criminal deals. It is not impossible that members of these groups abused their official position, although there is no proof either for or against this supposition. And how can there be? Theoretically, a totalitarian economy can "feed" whole clans through illegal business. Together with dedicated Stalinists, it was these clans that were the regime's mainstay.

Stalinism and socialism also generated another curious phenomenon, a difference between official unearned and unofficial earned incomes. The former include the incomes derived as a result of a high social status (privileges, access to goods in short supply), and the latter, revenues yielded by "hidden economic activity". This is not an idle issue. The alleged ability of Stalinism to do away with the shadow activities and groups is a trump in the hands of those who are still advocating "the socialist choice". But, since proof is lacking, we shall have to let history pass its judgment. As for war communism introduced after the 1917 revolution, that was a time when a shadow economy not only existed but flourished.

The Illusions of Capitalism

The other extreme is the "capitalist choice". Capitalism is supposed to permit everything and turn the shadow economy into a piece of nonsense.

Illegal operations, income concealment, and criminal business (including drugs) are all significant elements of the world capitalist economy. For instance, a big bang in the West was made by the investigation into the activities of the Bank for International Credit and Commerce operating mainly with Arab money, which financed only criminal deals, such as arms trade and the narcobusiness. And many people in this country now believe in capitalism without a shadow economy more firmly than they used to believe in communism.

Some economists and writers insist that the shadow economy attracts only talented, vigorous entrepreneurs, and that if some of them are currently kept behind the bars, this is wrong. Let them do what they would under capitalism, and they would, allegedly, fill the shops with food and consumer goods. This view is more than debatable, resting as it does on the erroneous assumption that if a law is bad it may be ignored or violated. But the very chance to find a loophole in the law and emerge unscathed depends, not so much on personal daring, resourcefulness, and shrewdness as on other factors, namely, a having a good cover and knowing the right people. The reference is to direct contacts with the party and state bosses in the Soviet economic environment.

Our shadow dealers transgressed the boundaries of what was permitted not because of bureaucratic snags alone. This category of people included mostly criminal types, whose business was crooked to begin with.

Economic analysts of some national newspapers are now trying to prove that under capitalist market relations, corruption in the economy is impossible. However, if private businessmen of the 1970s practised capitalism under socialism, what was so praiseworthy about that? They did not make money because they won in an honest competition, as they would under capitalism, but simply because for a variety of reasons they had a chance to pull their illegal deals off. All their profits were purely criminal, derived as a result of artificial restriction of competition. In the West, monopoly and the profits obtained on its basis are penalized. The issue of unfair treatment of the shadow dealers in the Soviet Union simply does not arise, or there would be danger of deciding that capitalist laws are also bad, binding as they do someone's hands (which they do), and so need not be observed.

PARTNERSHIP AND RIVALRY

By 1985, the outset of perestroika, there existed in the USSR a system in which elements of the socialist regime "harmoniously blended" with essentially capitalist but illegal sources of wealth. There were groups that reflected different social interests: purely political groups, social strata (party and state nomenklatura, people working in wholesale and especially retail trade), ethnic clans, and sometimes purely corporate associations, like ministries and administrative departments. Their common features were a mixture of official and unofficial business and a bent towards extracting profits peculiar to this country alone: not money but greater nomenklatura and shadow influence used to enrich the group members by every available means.

It took very little cause for rivalry among these essentially unstable groups to flare up. Mainly, it centered around production matters, distribution of imported goods, foreign-trade export licenses, credits, taxation, domestic trade funds, and investments into construction and the agro-industrial complex. True, one does not want to exaggerate and dump together the formal bureaucratic hierarchy of the Communist Party and the shadow mafia-type networks, as some authors are prone to do. Others talk about "interest parties", extending this phenomenon to broad strata of people on the basis of regional and sectoral criteria. This approach is open to criticism. In a totalitarian state, a rank-and-file jobholder is so far alienated from property that the very discussion of real interests of millions of people is pointless.

As Soviet society moved on, more and more sophisticated and complex methods of struggle and competition were used in the corridors of power. In principle, the rivalry was of long standing, and not only among the factions inside the Politburo and the Party Central Committee, or between the KGB and the Ministry for Internal Affairs. The competition became so tangled and produced such a ramified non-formal network of relations that new economic methods had to be used. In principle, only by connecting the evolution of official economic reforms declared at the Communist Party congresses with the changes in the place and role of the various shadow economy groups can one comprehend what was going on in 1985-1991 in politics and the economy. The pace of changes in the structure of official and "shadow" relations increased, and the race went to the swifter and tougher contestants. Both the underground businessman and their patrons at various levels were obliged to adapt to each economic innovation, to put them to use in the competitive struggle. This pertains to the zones of influence and the functions of individual state bodies and departments, for which reason the struggle shifted from one sphere to another.

The Regional Aspect

To realize that the shadow economy is a mirror reflection of the legal economy and that it is "socialist" and "Soviet" by nature, it is enough to analyze the overall trend of its evolution. There were, of course, regional distinctions. In Central Asia, total corruption and the rule of a hierarchical system of control had strong local features. In the Transcaucasus, the stealing was more shameless, as there existed firm guarantees of mutual covering up. In the Ukraine and Moldavia, the "shadow" aspects of life were carefully hidden from the public.

Russia and the Baltics stood apart. In the latter, the shadow economy did not spread very far, probably because legal entrepreneurial initiative still survived from 1945, when socialism triumphed there. Also, the locals there were more law-abiding than elsewhere in the Soviet Union. As for Russia, it gradually shaped a corrupt system of political and economic power that was all its own, but since the republics were economically bound together, the sectoral structure was not uniform, and the shadow economy stood at different development levels, there appeared adverse trends that have made themselves felt only recently. I refer to the structure of economic relations that was very unfavorable for Russia, fettered it hand and foot, and was gradually ruining it.

The raw-materials appendages, the extracting industries found themselves serving the manufacturing ones, as it was at the stage of manufacturing that "shadow" economic elements appeared, which later grew into underground workshops and whole factories. The mechanisms of thefts at the extracting stage, as well as in construction, was geared at obtaining more money, equipment, materials, and imported goods than was required, and capitalized on wastefulness, incomplete and dragged-out projects and overstating the cost of works. In agriculture, the chief stake was made on "natural" losses and write-ups (distorting data in reports by exaggeration upwards). The shadow transport network had methods and techniques of its own.

So it is a big mistake to think that under the old system, the chief thieves were working in retail trade: the latter were simply more in the public eye. Much bigger thefts were performed in, say, the agro-industrial complex, in construction, and in the state allocation system, such as the State Committee for Supplies and the State Planning Committee, where the expenses were hard to monitor, or in the Ministry for Fish Industry and in the Ministry of Water Supplies (suffice it to recollect the well-known "fish case"). The State Committee for Petroleum Products had evolved a nationwide system of stealing fuel, which culminated in the notorious trial involving the minister himself.

Different republics had different sectoral structures: this has to be considered when tracing the spread of "shadow" processes. The allocation of resources and investments was controlled by a shadow network. And now the government that has recently come to power is trying to find out why the structure of the economic sectors and links, especially in foreign trade, finances, and investments is so prejudicial to Russia's interests. The young industrial ministers, enamored though they are of Milton Friedman's economic theory, must have missed his work devoted exclusively to the shadow economy. This, I believe, is their biggest mistake.

EMERGING FROM THE SHADOW

The shadow economy, organized crime, and the mafia played a part at each stage of perestroika and economic reform of the past few years. In 1985-1987, the prevalent orientation was at the state sector and corresponding methods of sharing the pie. The declared "campaigns", "courses", and "programs" in actual fact disguised the shadow tycoons' claims for raw materials, money, equipment, and investments formulated at the lower levels of the corrupt apparatus. For instance, a line at "accelerated" or "priority" development of one industry or another would be declared, providing an opportunity to get additional investments and other boons. Frequent use was made of the so-called "experimental" method (this continued up to 1990), under which an enterprise or a group of enterprises were granted economically unjustified privileges. The Law on Cooperation, which, in fact, triggered off the chaos of recent economic reforms, did not really pursue the goals its authors, most probably honest people all of them, intended it to. The powers that be used the "Potyomkin village" cooperatives to launder their dirty money.

This is the reason why in 1987-1988, first fiddle in most cooperatives was played by shadow economy dealers. The choice of the spheres where to apply "shadow" capital could not be better. Sales of shish-kebab in street kiosks complemented the long-established crooked business at the meat product factories, the clothes-making co-ops were used by the managers of underground clothes-making factories, former bribe-takers in public catering and retail trade began to open cooperative cafes and shops.

All this does not mean that honest and enterprising people were non-existent. Many production and building co-ops were doing a useful job. But by and large, the mafia snatched the chance to legalize part of its business and to launder their ill-gotten money.

What happened next? In 1988, unrest began in the foreign economic sphere, which had used to be airtight before. What was going on in it is still a mystery for the public. It would take a special study to examine the shadow side of international and foreign economic links.

The only thing that needs mentioning is that the mafia was galvanized into action by the smell of hard currency. Very big money was now involved. Commercial banks began to mushroom, the financial circles began to play a part, and the field of operation broadened. Top-ranking apparatchiks, who used to extract tribute from private business, began to take a direct part through a streamlined racket ran by the KGB and Ministry for Internal Affairs. These two organizations either had those who refused to pay or did not pay enough arrested, or sent hired assassins supplied by the mafia, which had close contacts with the law-enforcement bodies.

Since 1988, the development of capitalism in Russian entered a new stage. Apparatchiks began to get jobs with joint ventures and commercial banks for their children and to set up "legal" businesses using their far-flung contacts and extensive opportunities. By that time, the old and no longer necessary nomenklatura had been got rid of: nearly all these people lost their jobs in 1986-1987. The new leaders intended to stay in power for a long time. One of the reasons why the "nomenklatura" joint ventures, commercial banks, and cooperatives stepped up their activities was the fact that by 1988, the mafia proper had consolidated its financial status and was now hard to control by old, time-tested methods. And so it all began.

The plum was, of course, foreign trade. Raw materials were pumped West through joint ventures. Remnants of raw materials, secondary raw materials, and other export commodities appeared as if by miracle. Since direct involvement was still risky, the big operations were conducted by intermediaries, like the Tekhnika cooperative headed by Artem Tarasov or, later, the state-cooperative ANT concern.

Quite a few new businessmen managed to use trendy verbiage to pull off lucrative deals. The shadow circles made the first serious attempt to legalize the money made in this way in late 1988-early 1989, when as a result of the clash between two competing bureaucratic economic groups the proscenium was taken by Artem

Tarasov. The reconnaissance was, for the most part, successful. Later, Tarasov was elected People's Deputy of the RSFSR and even began to work on "programs" of the Russian government, that is, pump Soviet oil to the West. The outcome of that affair is known well enough. In the spring of 1991, Tarasov decided to stop tempting fate. But he "awakened" the still slumbering top of the ruling nomenklatura.

Since the summer of 1990, this process has had a much more terrifying aspect. The party and government nomenklatura "joined in the fun", quickly leaving the mafia, the cooperative dealers, and even joint ventures and commercial banks far behind.

The stakes were now very high. The large economic administrative bodies began to metamorphose, at varying speeds, into commercial establishments. The State Committee for Supplies evolved into a network of commodity exchanges, which explains why we have so many of them and why they are making so much money. Enterprises and companies began to ignore the State Planning Committee and conclude barter deals and make direct contacts. As a result, the profits settled no one knows where.

The system of foreign trade was rapidly falling apart. But the companies set up by its former employees were doing extremely well. A prominent part was performed by the military-industrial complex and the KGB. The former had the material basis, and the latter began to plant its agents in the commercial network. And as before, the process was directed from Old Square, the seat of the Communist Party Central Committee.

A special place belonged to the so-called "conversion" deals. Highly corrupt groups connected with the State Bank and the Foreign Economic Bank sprang up in this sphere. The Finance Ministry and the State Bank launched a campaign to set up a stock market. The country's leadership planned to accomplish this feat before large-scale privatization was announced. The "500 days" program was rejected precisely because too many members of the nomenklatura had not yet created a niche in the "invisible" economy for themselves. That was the cause of the failure, not Ryzhkov's supposed differences with the authors on points of theory.

By mid-1991, the efforts of the new prime minister, Valentin Pavlov, culminated in a powerful program of transition from socialism to capitalism controlled by the party and state apparatus and with the latter's subsequent rule as the new bourgeoisie. By that time, the mafia, as well as the joint ventures and cooperatives that flourished at the first stage of perestroika were already pushed back to roughly the same positions in the shadow or invisible economy they had occupied before 1987.

The stage was set, it only remained to legalize the transition to market relations under this scheme, declare themselves entrepreneurs, businessmen, capitalists, and conduct a powerful propaganda campaign. The press and television were full of business, businessmen, people with initiative, brainwashing the public into seeing them as society's saviors. The mass media acted in all good faith and were quite right. But what did the words actually disguise? Real estate had already been divided, billion-rouble contracts signed, and the best enterprises sold in advance. Mighty cohorts of industrial tycoons made political debuts. Contrary to what many people believe, underhand, barbaric privatization began not after August 19 but a year earlier.

What can be done now? How does one draw a line between what is right and legal, and what is harmful and even criminal? The reference is not just to the coup and its organizers. The country contains too many potential economic transgressors whose future depends on the practical terms into which the theoretical disputes about the ways and methods of privatization will be translated. The decisions must consider, above all else, the interests of the millions of "ordinary" people. In the past year, the country's "capitalizers" got carried away and forgot that splitting comes after creating, not the other way around.

This is why the subject of the "shadow economy" disappeared from the pages of newspapers. Economics, right, and ethics became mixed up. What will outweigh the rest: economic pragmatism, legal nihilism, or moral romanticism? One thing is, however, clear: nothing can be worse than violence, and this is why we need a round table, this time not in politics but in economics.

Subject Index